Listening To God

Listening To God

Joyce Huggett

HODDER AND STOUGHTON
LONDON SYDNEY AUCKLAND TORONTO

The quotation from PRAYERS OF LIFE by Michel Quoist is reproduced by courtesy of the publishers, Gill and Macmillan.

Bible quotations are from the New International Version.

British Library Cataloguing in Publication Data

Huggett, Joyce
  Listening to God.
  1. Christian life
  I. Title
  248.4   BV4501.2

ISBN 0 340 39274 6

Hodder and Stoughton Editorial Office: 47 Bedford Square, London WC1B 3DP

For Andrew, whose friendship I value, whose experience of God whets my appetite all over again and whose adventure into prayer is both an inspiration and joy to watch.

And in memory of Tom, who first taught me to listen to God.

Contents

Acknowledgements

Countless people have contributed to this book in one way or another. Most of them remain blissfully ignorant of that fact. Nevertheless I would like to express my thanks to a few of them.

I shall always be indebted to the monks of Mount St Bernard Abbey whose life and witness and worship made such a major contribution to my early explorations into contemplative prayer. I shall always be grateful, too, to the sisters of St Hilda's Priory in Whitby who welcomed me into their fold with such warmth and generosity even though I was a complete stranger. And my very special thanks to the Sisters of the Love of God, particularly certain sisters at Boxmoor, who have offered me, not simply endless support in the pilgrimage of prayer, but lasting friendship also.

The Rt. Revd. Stephen Verney, the Bishop of Repton, has been a constant source of inspiration and encouragement. The members of the original prayer group at St Nicholas' Church, Nottingham, similarly shaped my prayer life. While thanking them, I must include, too, my husband and children who sacrificed family togetherness time to set me free to adventure into listening prayer and who also helped me to evaluate my findings.

Twelve people prayed for me while I was giving birth to this book. Without their love and intercessory prayer this book would never have been completed and I am glad of this opportunity to thank them publicly. Carolyn

Armitage, my editor, is someone whose wisdom, insights
and concern I have grown to value through the writing of
this book and to her I give another verbal bouquet. As for
my typist and friend, Joan Edlin, I cannot thank her
enough for typing and re-typing the manuscript without
complaint and for the endless encouragement she gives
me.

Preface

The prophet Amos once warned that the day would come when a famine would afflict God's people. This famine would not be a lack of bread nor a thirst for water. Rather, it would be a famine of *hearing* the words of the Lord: 'Men will stagger from sea to sea and wander from north to east, searching for the word of the Lord, but they will not find it' (Amos 8:12). Many Christians, myself included, believe that that prophecy has been fulfilled both in times past and in our own life-time. For generations, the ability to listen to God's still, small voice has waned. Even the desire to tune in to Heaven has vanished.

But there are definite signs to suggest that, during the past two decades, the tide has been on the turn. Now it seems to be coming in, sweeping across our country with increasing force and bringing in its wake a renewed hunger to hear God's voice and an insatiable thirst for the stillness which is pregnant with God's presence. For this reason retreats are 'in'. Guest houses in monasteries and convents are full of people anxious to withdraw from the rush and tumble of twentieth-century life, equally anxious to drop into the presence of God which they believe they might find in such a place.

In the autumn of 1976, this wave of the Spirit of God, for such I believe it is, swept over me. I did not ask for it. It just came. It swept me off my feet and the direction of my life was changed: not dramatically, but slowly, gradually, at times almost imperceptibly.

The immediate and chief change concerned my prayer life. From early childhood, prayer played a significant part in my life. But in 1976 a whole new dimension of this relationship with God opened up for me.

Before 1976, I had seen prayer as a duty to be performed and a place of refuge for me where I could pour out my needs to God and bring to him the needs of the world. When God mastered my life, touching it afresh with his almighty finger, to borrow Gerard Manley Hopkins'[1] imagery, that view changed. Prayer, I suddenly saw, is a gift given by God through his Holy Spirit. This gift comes, not as a reward for a life well-lived, not because we have earned it in any way, but as a tangible sign of God's grace: a gift of undeserved and unearned love.

I wish I could look back over the past nine years and record that they have been years of unmitigated joy as I have explored this precious gift. Alas! That is not my experience. What I can more truthfully say is that, with varying degrees of enthusiasm and commitment, for the past nine years I have *attempted* to unpack this gift. Sometimes, in doing so, I have experienced ecstasy, an indescribable joy, a sense of loving and being loved by God such as I never dreamed possible. At other times, I seemed to meet only darkness, pain and my own disobedience.

Nevertheless, for me, prayer has become a passion, a life-long quest, a journey, even an adventure. When I step off the path to take an excursion into a cul-de-sac dissatisfaction creeps over me and I find myself scampering back to this path of prayer once more. When the path becomes obscured with the overgrowth of my own waywardness, God in his mercy comes to hack a way through the brambles, to set me on the way again. Only then is my heart-hunger satisfied.

To write about one's own prayer pilgrimage must, by nature of the assignment, be costly. I, at least, have found the writing of this personal pilgrimage of prayer a costly privilege.

Why stand before the world spiritually naked? Why make yourself vulnerable in this way? the reader might well ask. I cannot speak for others who write about prayer. I can speak for myself. There are two reasons why I decided to put pen to paper on this subject. One is because I meet so many people, young Christians in particular, who are asking the kind of questions I was asking nine years ago: Does God speak today as he did in Bible times? If so, *how* does he speak? How do I know whether it is his voice I have heard? What must I do if I would learn to tune in to God's still, small voice? This book is written with such people in mind. It is offered with the sincere prayer that they will find the answers to some of their questions in the pages that follow. It is offered because, deep down in my heart, a conviction has taken root that God still speaks today and he is actively seeking Christian people who will take his command to listen seriously.

The second reason why I took the plunge and decided to write about listening to God was that I sensed God himself was asking me to draw together three threads of spirituality which, at certain stages of the history of the church, seemed unlikely bed-fellows, even incompatible, but which the Holy Spirit of God seems, in recent years, to be weaving together in the lives of many Christians. I speak of the richness of the evangelical tradition with its faithfulness to the Word of God, the Bible, charismatic renewal, with its open-ness to the energising and empowering of God's Holy Spirit, and the contemplative life with its emphasis on encountering God and being encountered by him, rather than talking about God or merely meditating on thoughts about him.

In this book I describe how these three threads are being intertwined in my own life. I tell of some of the joys, some of the sorrows and some of the surprises that met me as this work of God began in my life nine years ago, and has since continued.

What I did not know as, with a certain naiveté, I

abandoned myself to this work of God's Spirit, was that he was working in a similar way in the lives of many other people, some of whom are now my friends. What I did not know at the time was that they, too, were wondering whether these strands *could* be woven together in one life so that God could make of these strands a strong rope of spirituality in one and the same person. But now I do know these facts because people to-day are brave enough to draw back the curtains and to allow others to catch a glimpse of God at work in the inner recesses of their lives.

There is a sense, then, in which this book is about reconciliation. It is an attempt to show how, in one life, *my* life, God is breaking down the barriers of suspicion and prejudice that divide Christian from Christian; how he seems to be impressing on me the fact that Christians in many camps not only have much to teach one another but they actually need each other if they are to become whole. I offer the book to readers in whom the Holy Spirit of God is working similarly with the encouragement not to fear the strange changes you may find happening to you, but to rejoice in them. For God invites us, not to stagnate in our spiritual life, but to change and to go on being changed.

I offer this book falteringly because of its biographical nature. One of my fears surrounding this piece of personal exposure was penned so well by C. S. Lewis:

> Those like myself whose imagination far exceeds their obedience are subject to a just penalty; we easily imagine conditions far higher than we have really reached. If we describe what we have imagined we may make others, and make ourselves, believe that we have really been there – and so deceive both them and ourselves.[2]

I have tried, in this book, to weigh those words; not to deceive myself or my reader, but to describe accurately what I discern. I offer the outcome prayerfully: my prayer

is that this book may become a bridge on which the
Christian earnestly desiring to hear God's voice and the
God who yearns to communicate with his children may
meet, embrace and encounter one another in listening
love.

JOYCE HUGGETT
Nottingham
1985

Chapter 1

Learning to Listen

Prayer became the warp and woof of my life very early on in my childhood. My father wove the first prayer-threads into the fabric of my experience. It was not that he taught me prayers, nor that he prayed with me, so far as I can remember. Instead, he taught me the value of prayer by allowing me to watch *him* at prayer.

I can see him now. Every evening, after work, he would settle himself into the armchair next to the coal fire which always blazed in the hearth of our tiny living room in winter. He would read the local newspaper from cover to cover, listen to the news on the wireless, then reach for his big, black, gilt-edged, leather-bound Bible. I would watch him out of the corner of my eye. I loved the smell of that leather and the rustle of the India paper and the shimmer of the gold pages. And I loved the look on my father's face as he read this treasured book. Reading it seemed to bring him contentment and joy even when times were hard, like when he was made redundant. When he had finished reading the Bible and the notes, I knew what he would do next. He would hand the Bible to my mother who sat in the armchair at the other side of the fire. While she flicked through the pages, he would close his eyes, bow his head and bury his apple-red face in one hand. And often I would contemplate his wavy, auburn hair and sit very still while I watched his thin lips move. Even when I was very young, I understood that at such moments I was not to interrupt. But when he lifted his head again, I would sometimes climb on his knee, snuggle into his arms and play with his floppy ear-lobes before giving him a smacking kiss on the cheek nearest the fire: the cheek which would be warm.

Our terraced house boasted only two bedrooms. My brothers shared one and I slept on a child-size bed in the corner of the other, sharing it with my parents. Often, I would still be awake when my parents came to bed and I would watch as my mother folded back the flamingo-pink satin bedspread before kneeling with my father on the cold, pink lino beside their bed. My father would frequently linger in this attitude of prayer and again, I would study his prayerful form and watch the silent movement of his lips.

Children are great imitators of people they love. Perhaps it is not surprising, then, that I cannot remember a time when prayer did not feature in my life.

Among my earliest memories is a picture of myself kneeling by *my* bed in prayer and the recollection of a regular routine. I would lie in bed with the light on and sing at the top of my voice until someone came to tell me to stop. My favourite song was one my father taught me and which we used to sing in Sunday school:

> It is a thing most wonderful
> Almost too wonderful to be
> That God's own Son should come from heaven
> And die to save a child like me.
>
> I sometimes think about the cross
> And shut my eyes and try to see
> The cruel nails and crown of thorns
> And Jesus crucified for me.

And I would close my eyes, visualise Jesus hanging on the cross, and my heart would be strangely warmed. God's love for me caused a stirring in my heart. Even at a tender age I wanted to respond by giving him the love that welled up inside me as I thought of him hanging on the tree for me.

By the time I reached my teens, a personal pattern of prayer was well established. Every evening, like my father, I would read the Bible, study the passage with the aid of Scripture Union notes and kneel beside my bed to pray. The deepest desire of my heart was to live life God's way. But what was God's way?

I remember puzzling over this when I fell in love for the first time. I was fourteen and my hero was an athletic fifteen-year-old. He would meet me from school and we would cycle home together and kiss and cuddle in the park near my home. No one ever talked to me about the ecstasy of falling in love. No one ever explained to me how a Christian should behave with members of the opposite sex, so even though I enjoyed the kissing and the cuddling, at the same time I was anxious. The only person I talked to about the situation was God. He had my complete confidence. At night I would kneel by my bed and tell him everything. And I would ask him a whole string of questions: Is it right to feel this way about a boy? Is it wrong to do these things in the park? Is this partner the one you want me to marry? My heart was full of trust and sincerity as I unburdened myself. The problem was that no answer came. I would rise from my knees as perplexed as before.

The same ceiling of silence met me when another boyfriend asked me to marry him. I was eighteen at the time and working hard at my 'A' levels. I remember being flattered and confused, stunned and excited all at the same time. Unable to talk to my parents about such things, I knelt in my usual spot that night – on the rug beside my bed – and begged God to show me what I should say to this infatuated young man. No audible answer came. Only silence.

Throughout my student days, the love of God drew me irresistibly. Prayer intrigued me, attracted me, and occupied several hours of my time each week. As a theology student I was obliged to study Church history. I envied the early monks and hermits I read about who had devoted their entire life to prayer. But I never discovered the secret of how to hear God. Neither did I meet anyone else who had learned this art. Prayer, for me, was like a telephone conversation where one person did all the talking. I was that person. I seem to remember being taught that prayer was the way man communicated with God. Bible reading was the way God chose to speak to man.

Whether I was actually taught that or not, this was what I believed and each day I would make time both to talk to God and to try to listen to him by reading the Bible. One of my tutors in the Theology Department discovered this personal pattern of prayer. It earned me and others like me the label 'God-botherers'. But we didn't mind. Prayer mattered.

From our honeymoon on, my husband and I prayed together as well as apart. In prayer, we would chatter away to God. When we needed an answer to an urgent question we would hope that a verse from the Bible would leap out from the page and point us in the right direction, or that circumstances and the advice of friends would coincide and that in this way God would make his will clear.

When our son was born, we taught him to pray. When our daughter arrived, we prayed over her and with her and for her. While I breast-fed her in the early hours of the morning, I would enjoy the stillness and pray. Prayer was one of the pivotal experiences of our family life. Yet prayer somehow created a hunger. It was as though a whole piece of the jig-saw was missing.

Listening to God
When our son was eleven years old, my husband accepted a

job in Nottingham. He was to pastor a church in the centre of the city. Our new home would border the city's busy inner by-pass at the front and Woolworth's at the back. 'It's ideally situated for lunch-time meetings for business-men,' we decided before we even settled in.

Every Wednesday lunch-time, a handful of businessmen would meet in our lounge, drink soup, eat sandwiches, listen to a talk and pray. One of the most regular attenders was a retired member of our own congregation: Tom. From time to time, members of the group would lead the meeting for themselves rather than invite an outside speaker to address them. Whenever Tom's turn came round he would speak about a dimension of prayer he called 'listening to God'. He would insist that when a person listens to God, God speaks, and when a man obeys, God works.

Tom once described how this process of listening to God had turned his marriage inside out. While listening to God on one occasion, he sensed that God was urging him to ask his wife's forgiveness for the way he had failed in the past. That night, he made his confession and suggested that he and his wife should be quiet together. The result of this act of obedience was that his wife re-dedicated her life to Christ.

From that time on, Tom and his wife set the alarm for 6 a.m. every morning so that they could enjoy a time of quiet together. They would read the Bible, pray and listen for God's still, small voice. Whenever they sensed God was speaking to them, they would write down the instructions or challenges or directions they received. They determined to obey to the best of their ability. Because of this re-kindling of spiritual awareness, life opened up for them in a new way. The life and standards of Jesus became the pattern on which they cut their lives. Their love for one another deepened, their marriage was enriched, and the new quality of their lives touched their many friends and acquaintances.

Tom also described how during his times of attentive listening to God, creativity flowed and plans were hatched. On one occasion, he came to God burdened about the strike action which was paralysing the printing firm of which he was a director. God seemed to implant in his mind, not only a method to end the strike, but ideas which, when implemented, created a new spirit in the firm. On another occasion God seemed to place a burden on his heart for a Marxist friend of his. During his early morning period of quiet, ideas flowed which, when put into practice, resulted in this man's conversion to Christ.

Tom's testimony both fascinated and frightened me. I admired Tom. Kindness overflowed from him and his wife to my family and me. His genuineness, honesty and transparency could not be denied. But although I detected a fluttering of desire in the pit of my stomach whenever he described his experience of detecting God's still, small voice, a certain memory filled me with dread and blocked the path of progress for me. Indeed, I shuddered as I recalled the tragedy of Jim, a friend of ours, who mistook wishful thinking for God's whisper.

Jim had been an undergraduate with my husband and me. We knew him well. Just after our wedding, he wrote to us to tell us that God had told him to marry a mutual friend of ours, another fellow undergraduate, Jenny. 'But that's stupid,' I protested when I read the letter. 'Jenny's engaged to Geoff. They're getting married in three months' time.' We resisted responding to Jim's letter. Jenny married Geoff. Several months later, another letter arrived from Jim insisting that God had told him to marry Jenny. This time, David, my husband, wrote to Jim to break the news. Jenny was married.

Undaunted, Jim jumped on the next train and came to our home protesting that Jenny had made a mistake. Indeed, at first he refused to believe that Jenny was married. Only after inspecting the marriage register in the church where the wedding had taken place was he convinced that Jenny was now committed to Geoff 'for better, for worse'.

Jim's reaction strained our own relationship with him and brought considerable distress to the newly-weds, Jenny and Geoff. The recollection of this distressing incident caused me to question whether Tom's apparent hot-line to God was authentic. I could tell that it was important to him, but I was not convinced that the Bible encouraged us to listen to God in this way and so, somewhat reluctantly, I dismissed his prayer recipe, and was even slightly suspicious of it.

God has his own way of breaking through our personal prejudices. Francis Thompson's poem, *The Hound of Heaven*, a favourite poem of mine, reminds us of this glad fact:

> I fled Him, down the nights and down the days;
> I fled Him, down the arches of the years;
> I fled Him, down the labyrinthine ways
> of my own mind, and in the mist of tears
> I hid from Him . . .
> From those strong Feet that followed, followed after.[1]

I was not aware when I discounted Tom's experience of listening to God that I, too, was a would-be escapee. But it seems that that is how God saw me. And, as always, the hound of heaven pursued gently, sensitively, persistently. Once again, he conquered. But this time, *I* became his willing victim.

Chapter 2

Tuning in to God

By this time the city centre church where we were working and worshipping was humming with new life. One reason for this was the influx of students who worshipped with us on Sundays. They came from Nottingham University and the polytechnic. In the autumn of 1976, two years after our arrival in Nottingham, the chaplain of the poly invited us to attend a weekend conference which he was organising for some of his students and to speak to them on the subject of prayer. 'We'll be holding the conference at Mount St Bernard Abbey,' he explained. 'It's a Roman Catholic monastery about forty minutes' drive from Nottingham.'

David and I each prepared our talks and duly arrived at the monastery. I had never darkened the doors of a monastery before, but as we entered the tree-lined drive, I remember smiling at our arrogance. 'Why on earth have *we* come to do the speaking?' I asked David. 'These monks have given their lives over to the work of prayer. Surely they know more about it than we do?'

I was to speak first. A white-robed, bald-headed monk sat at the back of the meeting and from time to time I wondered what his evaluation of my lecture would be. When the students broke up into small discussion groups, therefore, I engineered the grouping to ensure that I sat in the same group as this expert on prayer. I was eager to hear what he would say.

The aim of the discussion was to encourage each person to explain to the others the methods of prayer which had proved beneficial to them. The monk listened, nodding and smiling from time to time, but not speaking. Towards the end of the discussion we invited him to divulge the secret of his prayer life. His reply was to haunt me for weeks. 'Oh,' he replied, his eyes twinkling merrily as he spoke, 'I find that a rather difficult assignment. You see, most of my praying these days is done in silence.' I failed utterly to understand how someone could spend most of their life in prayer and yet by-pass words. The mystery of this statement bothered me every time I thought about it in the weeks that lay ahead.

The monk befriended my husband and me that day and planted a suggestion in our minds.

'Why don't you come here and make a retreat on your own one day?' The very phraseology, 'make a retreat', sounded suspiciously Catholic to our Protestant ears, but something about this prayer sanctuary had hooked us. Early in December, we arrived to make our first retreat.

I shall never forget that first sip of real stillness. The retreat demanded nothing of us except simply to be in the presence of God. Coming, as we had, straight from the activism of parish life in a busy city-centre church, this absence of the driving need to achieve was therapy in itself. The monastery, with its prayer-saturated walls and fabric, its quiet rhythm and its God-centredness, seemed to us a welcome oasis. We were being nourished, renewed and refreshed. We each rejoiced to watch the other relax in the warmth of the felt love of Christ, a phenomenon which seemed rare at home.

From time to time during our forty-eight hour retreat, the monk met us and explained some of the mysteries of his experience of prayer. He also lent us a book which was to change my life. As I read John Powell's, *He Touched Me*, I was deeply moved. Here was a man who understood my quest, who voiced my struggles, and who was unafraid to expose his personal vulnerability by expressing how he had stumbled across answers to the kind of questions I had been asking.

How does God communicate himself to me? How does he disclose who he is after I have revealed myself to him? Do I have to wait hours, days, weeks or even years to see what God will do with and about my open-ness to him? Or is there a more immediate and direct response? . . . Can God put a new idea directly and immediately into my *mind*? Can he give me a new perspective in which to view my life with its successes and failures, agonies and ecstasies? Can God put new desires into my *heart*, new strength into my *will*? Can he touch and calm my turbulent *emotions*? Can he actually whisper words to the listening ears of my soul through the inner faculty of my *imagination*? Can God stimulate certain *memories* stored within the human brain at the time these memories are needed?[1]

I had never had the courage to voice questions like these even though they had burned in my heart every time Tom talked to me about listening to God. With eagerness, I read on. John Powell's conclusion filled me with child-like excitements:

Of course I feel sure that God can and does teach us in these ways. I think of the whole Bible as simply a written record of such religious experience, of God invading human history and human lives, of God speaking to men. I also believe that this God is available and anxious to speak to you and me. Yes, just as anxious as he was to speak to Abraham, Isaac and Jacob, Isaiah and Jeremiah.[2]

'But would he come to me?' This question penned by John Powell also found an echo in my own heart. His testimony left me with an insatiable thirst:

> The Lord . . . puts his ideas into my mind, and especially
> his perspectives. He widens my vision, helps me to see
> what is really important in life, and to distinguish the
> really important from the unimportant . . . He comes to
> me, in the listening, receptive moments of prayer, and
> he transfuses his power into me.[3]

This man had an experience of prayer which was like a
foreign language to me. I determined to learn that
language. I wanted what he had found and I was prepared
to make sacrifices for this pearl of great price.

The finger of God

Just as the father detected the early stirrings in the heart of
the prodigal son, it seems that God's all-seeing eye took
note of my fresh longings for him. He made an entry into
my life in a dramatic, gentle and sensitive way.

For eight years I had fought against the charismatic
movement. Its extremes and eccentricities disturbed and
alarmed me and I determined to steer clear of what seemed
to me mere emotionalism. But two weeks after this retreat
at Mount St Bernard Abbey, a trusted friend telephoned
late one night to tell me that he had been filled with the
Spirit and he thought he had been speaking in tongues. I
was angry. I remember the shudder which shook my
body as I noted the excitement in his voice. I recall my
response: 'Oh dear! Perhaps we should talk about this
after the meeting tomorrow night.' I did not give voice to
my determination to knock this nonsense out of his head,
neither did I react verbally to his parting comment: 'Joyce,
I think there's something in this for you.' But I dreaded
our encounter and hoped it would not mark the end of a
happy friendship.

After the meeting that Monday night, this member of
our congregation and I talked long and late. I knew him

well and I could not deny that God had touched him. It would be useless, I knew, to talk him out of a religious experience which had so clearly revitalised his love for God, renewed his thirst for Bible reading and empowered his prayer life. It was that night, as we prayed, that the hound of heaven caught up with me. I could no longer fight off the new surge of life with which he filled me. I have no words to describe what happened. I simply remember that I tingled with joy. The next day I was buoyant with this joy. As I put it to my husband, 'I suppose this is what it means to be filled with the Spirit of God.' I no longer felt hungry in prayer. I could not stop myself praying. I prayed as I walked to the shops. I prayed as I met the children from school. I prayed when I went to bed and when I got up in the morning. But the nature of the prayer had changed. It ceased to be a string of requests, a tirade of questionings, beseechings and plaguings. Instead, the sense of the presence of God's life within stunned me into silence. This awed silence gave birth to wordless praise, wordless adoration and wordless consecration of my life to him. Silence. Wordlessness. This was what the monk had been describing. A fresh touch from God. This was what John Powell had experienced.

The still, small voice

A dark-haired, brown-eyed school teacher we shall call Joan used to come to our home with a crowd of other young people most Sunday evenings at this stage of our church's history. She was shy and though I made several attempts to befriend her, I never felt I met the real person behind the dark eyes. When the phone rang one morning and Joan's voice cried out for help, I was surprised but pleased that she could trust me. Joan came round and explained that her mother had collapsed quite suddenly, that a diagnosis had been made and that she was suffering from a brain tumour which was thought to be incurable.

I felt helpless. After Joan left me, I asked God to heal this woman. Instead of promising to do that, I sensed that God was asking me to visit her in the nearby hospital. I am not claiming to have heard a voice. I did not. I am saying that an inner awareness which I shall refer to as a 'voice' spoke to me so clearly that I could not escape its implications. Indeed, it was so real that I argued with it. 'But, Lord, I don't even know her. What am I supposed to say?'

The voice simply replied, 'You go and I'll tell you what to say when you arrive.' The realisation that God wanted me to visit this sick woman would not go away. So I went.

As I walked through the hospital gates, my eyes lighted on a statue in the niche of a wall. The sculptor had chiselled out a sensitive representation of a shepherd holding a helpless lamb. The voice spoke again. 'Describe that statue to her.' In my faithlessness, again I protested. 'But, Lord, she's not a Christian. She won't understand what it means.' The reply came back. 'Never mind. Tell her.'

When eventually I found the patient, I talked to her about her illness, about her daughter, about the nurses. Just before I left, I described the statue I had seen. She listened, and seemed pleased that I had come, so I promised to return.

For several weeks, I visited this patient and a trusting friendship sprang up between us. Somehow I sensed that God was at work in her life. Even so, when she told me one afternoon that she was ready to die now that she knew the Good Shepherd for herself, I was stunned. She told me that she had thought a great deal about that statue and God had shown her himself through it. A few days later, she died.

This experience persuaded me that God can speak, that he does speak, and if we obey the inner prompting remarkable things can happen.

Another incident reinforced this realisation. A few weeks after Joan's mother's death, I received a phone call from a distressed clergy wife. She was dying of cancer and the treatment left her depressed and weak. I used to visit

her from time to time until she was hospitalised. Then I
wanted to avoid intruding on family visiting time, so I
simply prayed for her at home.

One afternoon, I could not get this woman out of my
mind. The voice I was learning to recognise as God's
pushed me into visiting her. As I sat by her bedside,
holding her bony, parchment-yellow hand, the same voice
whispered, 'Remind her of the hymn, "Just as I am".' My
reply shows how slow I was to learn to obey. 'But, Lord,
she's from a high-church tradition. She won't appreciate
that hymn.' The reply came. 'Never mind. Quote it.'

As I started the first line, I hoped I would be able to
remember the first verse. The whole hymn tumbled out of
my lips:

> Just as I am without one plea
> But that Thy blood was shed for me
> And that Thou bid'st me come to Thee
> O Lamb of God, I come . . .
>
> Just as I am, Thou wilt receive
> Wilt welcome, pardon, cleanse, relieve,
> Because Thy promise I believe
> O Lamb of God, I come.

When I had finished, her weak hand squeezed a thank
you and, quietly, I left.

A few days later, she died. When I attended the funeral, I
was startled to find that one of the hymns her husband had
chosen was this same hymn, 'Just as I am'. Later, he
explained. 'The words of that hymn brought her such
consolation and peace even in the middle of all the
suffering of the final pain-wracked hours on earth. She
would often ask me to read it to her.'

Again, I was deeply touched. I could no longer deny that
God speaks today.

In these action-packed weeks, I seemed to be discovering

for myself that Tom's claims were correct. The indwelling Spirit of God does speak today and he wants us to listen. What is more he wants us to act as well as hear. This discovery swung open a door into a whole new spiritual realm for me. Like Lucy in C. S. Lewis' book, *The Lion, the Witch and the Wardrobe*, I found myself in a world which was connected with our own but which was mysteriously other. Like Lucy, I was filled with wonder, awe, and spine-tingling excitement. I identified with the mixture of emotions C. S. Lewis describes when God surprised him by joy:

> I was overwhelmed . . . the long inhibition was over, the dry desert lay behind, I was off once more into the land of longing . . . There was nothing whatever to do about it: no question of returning to the desert. I had simply been ordered – or, rather, compelled – to 'take that look off my face.' And never to resume it either.[4]

Chapter 3

A Taste of Silence

Whenever I could I would go to Mount St Bernard Abbey to pray. Sometimes all I could spare would be a few hours. Sometimes I managed to stay for a whole day. Very occasionally I would make a retreat of thirty-six hours.

What was it that drew me? A recent visit helped me to pin-point the power of the place. I had driven through hazardous conditions to reach the abbey, along snow-packed lanes, through a blinding blizzard; on the way my car had skidded and in doing so had collided with another, bigger car. Even so, when eventually I had parked outside the abbey guest house, picked my way through ankle-deep snow-drifts and lifted the latch of the oak chapel door, I became aware of a peace invading my spirit.

The hush of the prayer-saturated chapel seeped into me. Within seconds, I had fallen to my knees, aware of my surroundings, the smell of fresh furniture polish, the sound of the monks shuffling into the choir stalls, the wind howling round the building, yet intensely aware of a love which drew me to itself, the love of God.

The sense of God's presence and love was so strong that it banished all memories of the traumatic journey. This love called from me a response. While the monks worshipped, like a sponge which had lain hard and shrivelled I opened every cell and fibre of my being to the warmth, the radiance and beckoning of the love of the living Lord.

'And this was how it always was,' I reflected. 'In this place the Lord calls me from my preoccupation with self and my overbusyness to focus on him and him only. In this place he touches me, the real me which often I hide from the world. He touches me through the winsomeness of the music, he touches me through the visual stimulus of the cross, he touches me through the powerful, prayerful atmosphere, he touches me through the flickering candle which somehow stills my harassed heart.'

When the monks left the church, I would linger there, as I did on this occasion. And I would be aware that every part of my being – body, mind and spirit – were open, attentive to the divine presence. I had done nothing to prepare myself for this eventuality. God had done it. The initiative was his. The miracle was his. By beaming his love on to me in a way I could feel, parts of me which normally remain closed, unfolded. I suppose I was rather like the water lily which opens itself when it can bask in warm sunshine but which closes its petals when cloud or rain obliterate the sun.

What I heard in those times of listening was more than a voice. It was a presence. Yes. I heard the Lord call my name. But I also 'heard' his tenderness. I soaked up his love. And this listening was on a level which runs deeper than mere words. Sometimes it seemed as though Jesus himself stood in front of me or beside me or above me. This encounter with him overwhelmed me. Was it his radiance? Was it the tenderness of his gaze? Or was it the fact of his gaze? The only way I can describe it is to liken it to the overwhelming a person feels when they love someone very deeply. That person's heart burns with pure pleasure at the joy of being in the presence of the loved one, that person's eyes sparkle or shine or mist over with warmth and deep-felt emotion, but that person does not speak. No words are necessary. They might even be intrusive for they could trivialise the love. And nothing must spoil the ecstasy of their encounter which may be all too brief in any case. They are content simply 'to be' in one another's presence. But that silence is packed with warm communication.

I had never delighted in God in this way before. And it had never occurred to me that God wanted me to linger in his presence so that he could show me that he delighted in me. Until now, my prayer had been vocal, busy, sometimes manipulative, always achievement-orientated. To kneel at the foot of a cross, allow music to wash over me so that I could 'just be' with God in a stillness which convinced me that 'he is', that 'he is God', was a new experience. But to 'waste time' for God in this way was changing my life, changing my view of God, changing my perception of prayer, changing my understanding of listening to God.

The problem was that, while I could achieve this kind of stillness in a place where people prayed day-in, day-out, I was married, the mother of two teenage children, heavily involved in helping my husband in a busy parish. I could never be a monk. I might fantasise about becoming a hermit, but my vocation, I realised, was not simply to prayer but to marriage, to motherhood, to service in the community. How was I to take what I experienced of God at Mount St Bernard Abbey and translate this into my everyday spiritual pilgrimage?

While I was still puzzling over this problem, glandular fever knocked me sideways. Perhaps it was God's way of giving me the time and space I needed to sift my priorities? Perhaps it was his opportunity to speak in tones I could not have detected had I been living life at the normal pace? C. S. Lewis rightly reminds us that pain is God's megaphone through which he speaks to a deaf world.

I do not know why this illness removed me from the front line of activity for months. What I do know is that a book which a friend gave me while I was ill presented me with the answer to my question, 'How can I draw near to

God in the busyness of my everyday routine?' It also answered another question which was bothering me at the time but which I had not yet had the courage to face. Was this facet of prayer, which no one had told me about before, and which I scarcely dared to mention in the circles in which I moved, simply an emotional, me-centred trip? Or was it a well-tried path of prayer of which I was so far ignorant?

The name of the book was *Poustinia* which, in Russian, means 'desert' or 'hermitage'. The author, Catherine de Hueck Doherty, was born in Russia but defected to the West after the October revolution in 1917. Eventually she settled in Canada where she began to teach spiritually hungry people an approach to God which had been her heritage in her homeland. Her thesis is that modern man needs silence just as much as his fore-fathers needed it:

> If we are to witness to Christ in today's market places, where there are constant demands on our whole person, we need silence. If we are to be always available, not only physically, but by empathy, sympathy, friendship, understanding and boundless *caritas*, we need silence. To be able to give joyous, unflagging hospitality, not only of house and food, but of mind, heart, body and soul, we need silence.[1]

This paragraph struck an immediate chord in my heart. And it was quickly followed by another observation which seemed to have been written just for me: "This silence is not the exclusive prerogative of monasteries or convents. This simple, prayerful silence is everybody's silence – or if it isn't, it should be.'[2] The author develops her thesis by explaining that a poustinia means a quiet, lonely place where people retreat because they desire to encounter God and because they seek to listen to him. She makes the claim that God reveals himself in a rare fullness to the person who withdraws from the maelstrom of life in this way. It is a place where we can be still and know that God is God, where God can fulfil his promise: 'I will lead her into the desert and speak tenderly to her' (Hos. 2:14).

I was lying in bed when I read this book. By the time I reached her practical suggestions about such a retreat place, I was sitting bolt upright from sheer enthusiasm. She emphasises that a poustinia need not be completely away from the haunts of men. Some people had reserved in their homes a small room to which they went to pray and meditate, which some might call a poustinia.

Within four months of reading this book, we had moved to a rambling four-storey house with seven bedrooms. Even before we moved, the attic-type bedroom at the top of the house was earmarked for silence. I would make it into a prayer room where I could adventure further into silence without having to withdraw from the family so frequently.

Going deeper

At this time, my friendship with the lady chaplain at Nottingham University took on a new significance. This friend was a nun, a sister on loan to the university from a convent in Whitby. She used to visit me as I recovered from glandular fever and we would talk about prayer, particularly silent prayer. With pride I showed her my prayer room tucked away at the top of the new house.

As the summer holidays approached, Sister Stella Mary prepared to spend the vacation back in the community. Just before she left Nottingham, she sprang an invitation on me: 'Why don't you come to Whitby for a few days while I'm there and taste *our* silence? The quiet of the convent and the sea air would do you good – hasten your healing.'

The idea attracted me for several reasons. First, I liked the idea of seeing this friend's 'home' for myself. Second, since it was an Anglican community, I knew I would be able to take communion there, something which I could not do at Mount St Bernard Abbey since I am not a Roman Catholic. Third, the thought of four days of solitude in congenial surroundings beckoned me after months of weariness and sickness.

My family warmed to the idea, too, so in August they drove me to the imposing grey stone castle now converted into a convent and a school.

I was spoiled: by God and by the sisters. For the four days I was there, the sun bathed the building and garden with warmth and light. I found a sun-drenched niche in the garden and there I sat, among the hollyhocks, with my back against the red brick wall and my face upturned to the sun, and for hour after hour I relaxed, read, drank in the peace, prayed and meditated on God's Word. From time to time I would relax, too, by striding along the seashore, watching the seagulls and envying their strength, but suddenly feeling as free as they looked. And I lapped up the kindness showered on me: like the day when I was observing total silence and a sister brought my coffee to the garden complete with home-made biscuits *and* a chocolate wrapped in gold foil.

But what made the most profound impact on me was the depth of the silence. I ate in the refectory with the sisters – in silence. I prayed in the chapel with the sisters each morning – in silence. Like them, I spent most of my day in silence.

I had never eaten in silence before. And I had never prayed with a group of people before without using any words. The power this silence generated stunned me.

Yes. I had sipped silence at Mount St Bernard Abbey, as I have said, and this had become precious. But Mount St Bernard Abbey flings wide its doors to people like me: people just beginning to explore the depths of prayer, people needing instruction, people needing help of varying kinds. Such people cannot sustain silence for long periods and so the peace of the place is punctuated by conversation in the guest house. From time to time noise pollutes the guest wing and it is probably appropriate that it should do so.

But here, at Whitby, guests do not disrupt the rhythm of the monastic way of life. They are fewer and they are absorbed by the community, its customs and its stillness.

This sustained stillness softened my spirit, making it receptive to the new seed-thoughts which were about to be sown.

Sister Stella Mary was shrewd. As we talked about God and about my longings for him, she detected that I was being called to contemplation. On the first evening of my visit, she lent me a book which I had never seen before, *Prayer and Contemplation* by Robert Llewellyn. It was another of those books which seemed to have been written especially for me.

From it, I learned that there is a close correlation between the charismatic experience which had crept up on me by surprise, and the yearning for solitude which I was currently experiencing. Robert Llewellyn explains that only the Holy Spirit can teach us how to pray. Indeed, prayer is his work within us. He is not only our teacher but our assistant. It is he who comes to help us in our weakness. When we are at a loss to know how to pray, 'the Spirit himself intercedes for us with groans that words cannot express' (Rom. 8:26). 'Groans that words cannot express', or as the RSV puts it, 'sighs too deep for words', or as one commentary paraphrases it, 'inexpressible longings which God alone understands'. This is one definition of contemplative prayer. Such contemplation is a gift of God's Spirit. Sometimes he teaches us to plumb the depths of silence. At other times he teaches us to vocalise spontaneous prayer. At other times again he encourages us to pray in tongues.

As I pondered on revelations like these, two thoughts struck me with the force of a flash of lightning. The first was that the kind of prayer which was drawing me again and again to Mount St Bernard Abbey had a name:

contemplation. The second was that this thing called contemplation was a gift God gave to his people through his Holy Spirit, a gift which enabled them to unfold to the presence of God.

With that intuitive knowing which is, of itself, a gift of God's Spirit, I knew that God was inviting me not simply to receive this gift but to unpack it; that he had brought me to Whitby with this primary purpose in mind.

This hunch was confirmed as I read more of Robert Llewellyn's book and particularly his description of the call to contemplation.

He suggests that it sometimes happens that a Christian is initiated into the life of prayer by learning to take a passage from the Bible, read it, examine it, ponder it, and consider how it affects his life-style and relationships with others. At the end of this period of Bible study, the person concerned will pray some kind of free, vocal prayer. I saw myself reflected in this description. It was the pattern I had practised for years.

He goes on to suggest that there may come a time when these occupations, though valuable in themselves, do no more than touch the fringe of our longing in prayer. They leave us with a sense of emptiness rather than fullness. Indeed, it becomes almost impossible to continue using these well-tried methods. What I read next persuaded me that God was trying to set my feet on a well-trodden path of prayer for which, as yet, I had no map, no compass, and no guide. Robert Llewellyn claims that when such changes are accompanied by a deep longing for God, when we find ourselves wanting him and him alone, then we may take this as a clear indication that the Holy Spirit is leading us into contemplative prayer. There is then only one option left: to yield to the impress of God's Spirit.

God used statements like these to show me his beckoning finger. Not knowing quite what I was surrendering to, since I had never consciously heard of contemplative prayer before, I said my 'Yes' to God. I wanted to be completely open to anything his Spirit had to give me.

Parched places inside me craved for more of the life-giving water of the Spirit which Robert Llewellyn implied was available. In the light of this I knew I could no longer be content with thoughts about God – either my own or other people's. I had to encounter him for myself; to meet him and be met by him. I could be content with nothing less. If necessary, I would go on making sacrifices for the privilege of pursuing this path of prayer. I was therefore ready to respond to God's further challenge:

Any who find within their hearts an answering cry to St Augustine's great words, 'Thou hast made us for thyself and the heart of man is restless till it finds its rest in thee,' and who are ready in the grace of God to face the testing experiences of the way, should go forward, nothing doubting, in the path which the Spirit is now calling.[3]

Chapter 4
Called to Contemplate

Refreshed, and in the full flush of joyful enthusiasm, I returned home. Contemplative prayer became a passion. My response to this call to contemplation was whole-hearted.

'Is there a technique for this kind of prayer, a kind of do-it-yourself guide to contemplation?' I wondered. If there was I was determined to unearth it.

Robert Llewellyn's book, which I had had to leave at the convent, had offered several hints to beginners. I had recorded many of these in the big, brown, battered exercise book I had taken to Whitby and which I now guarded with my life. Sister Stella Mary, too, sensing the spiritual metamorphosis which was taking place in me, was a walking warehouse of practical suggestions which she shared with me most generously. But she was in Whitby and I was in Nottingham. I needed a more permanent mentor and guide.

God has a marvellous way of bringing people, events and books into our lives just when we need them. As I stood at this cross-roads in my pilgrimage of prayer, my search for guidelines at its peak, another friend said to me one day, 'I thought you might be interested to take a peep at this.' 'This' was a booklet which she had borrowed from a friend. Its title *A Method of Contemplative Prayer* drew me in the same way as I imagine honeysuckle attracts bees on a summer's evening.

The author, James Borst, is a teacher of prayer who lives in India. I warmed to him immediately when I learned from the foreword to the booklet that, like me, he was a teacher and counsellor whose diary was so full that he had to create time to pray. And I felt further drawn to him when I read his own preface to the booklet. There he emphasises the two spiritual steps which had laid the foundations for his own prayer life: first, the step of accepting Jesus as his Lord and Saviour; second, the step of opening himself to an infilling of the Holy Spirit of God. He explains that this second step, for many people, is the open sesame to contemplative prayer; the beginning of a new life in the Spirit in which the love of God becomes an experienced reality rather than an acknowledged fact only.

I was eager for this new life in the Spirit, as I have said, so I thumbed through the pages of the sixty-page booklet. To my joy and astonishment, James Borst was applying himself to the self-same questions which were whirling round my brain: 'What is contemplation?'; 'How does one go about it?'; 'What does this kind of prayer achieve?'; 'How does it help us to listen to God?' A quick glance at the no-nonsense answers which the author offers in response to these questions persuaded me that this book was exactly what I needed at this stage of the prayer adventure.

Imagine my dismay when my friend explained that she had promised to return the book that evening and that I would not be able to buy a copy of my own because it was out of print. There and then I sat in her flat and copied out whole pages of the book in longhand. I knew I could not afford to allow such spritual gems to slip through my fingers.

The time was not wasted. As I wrote, my understanding of the nature of contemplative prayer deepened. I saw that contemplative prayer is essentially listening prayer. But it would not necessarily be words that I would be hearing. Rather, it would be an awareness of the presence of the indwelling Christ. I might start the prayer by using words like, 'Our Father in heaven'. But these words would not be the complete prayer. They would be like the sounding of a gong whetting my appetite and alerting me to the fact that the Father could be met and heard and loved. This broad definition of contemplative prayer was as tantalising to my spiritual palate as the smell of fresh ground coffee is to the natural taste buds. It reawakened the desire which had been quickened in me first at Mount St Bernard Abbey and then at Whitby.

With eagerness I noted the practical suggestions the author makes for those who respond to God.

A place and a time

The first requirement, he claims, is a place, preferably the privacy of one's own room. He reminds his readers of Jesus's example in this. Jesus himself 'often withdrew to lonely places and prayed' (Luke 5:16). And he recalls Jesus' exhortation: 'But when you pray, go into your room, close the door and pray to your Father, who is unseen' (Matt: 6:6).

I was privileged. My place was prepared. I read on. I wanted to know how I could make the best use of it.

He underlined the need we have to examine our commitments – family, profession, church, recreation – and within that framework to plot a daily appointment with God which we endeavour to keep as faithfully as possible. Progress would not be made in this pattern of prayer unless a definite time was fixed and kept, he claimed. Where possible, an hour a day should be set aside for this purpose.

A whole hour a day! As I looked at my diary, I wondered just where I could create an hour-long slot for prayer. But God challenged me through James Borst's observation,

'One full hour a day represents just about four per cent of all the time we live.'[1] Was I really saying that I could not consecrate four per cent of my life to attentiveness to God and him alone? Had I not noted in my exercise book:

> If we are called to contemplative prayer and are to respond to the Spirit's call, we must face the fact that this will call for sacrifice of time, for courage to persevere ... That is one side of the work, the side which is costly to the giver, and we may well ask, who is sufficient for these things?[2]

The least I could do was to try. At that time, my children were old enough to travel to school alone and my husband's office was not in our home as it normally is. By 8.30a.m. therefore a hush fell over our home after the early morning scurry to school and work. The best time to pray, I knew, would be from 8.30a.m. to 9.30a.m. If I earmarked that time for stillness before God I could be reasonably certain of being undisturbed. To guarantee this still further, I began to make it known in the parish that, except in emergencies, I would be grateful if phone calls could be delayed until after 9.30a.m.

To my surprise, people were not offended. They responded. This taught me two important lessons. If I am really serious about listening to God, I must fix my prayer time first and fit other things round it. If I am bold enough to make my plan public, others will support and encourage me in keeping my commitment.

Bodily posture

Just as a time and a place are basic to the life of prayer, so is attention to bodily posture. As I read this further claim in James Borst's booklet, I smiled. I had learned to pray from my father, as I have said. Copying him, and others whom I respected, usually when I prayed I would bend my body in two as though I had stomach cramp, and hold my head in my hands, a pious gesture which might have looked to the uninitiated onlooker as though I had a headache, or was trying to shield my eyes from the sting of shampoo, and to God may well have looked as though I was trying to hide from him rather than open myself to his love and his Word. But it had never occurred to me that the body can make a positive contribution to prayer, that different bodily postures correspond to different moods and emotions.

My mind went back to Whitby. There I had observed a woman stretched out on the floor, face down, lying prostrate, her arms held out, her body thus forming the shape of a cross. At first I had felt embarrassed. 'Was she all right? Would she mind someone seeing her in this position?' The more I thought about that woman at prayer: the harmony which was being expressed between her body and her spirit, the more profound the impact it made on me.

With James Borst's challenge came the desire to experiment. I would sometimes lie prostrate on my prayer room floor. I found that this bodily posture expressed penitence, unworthiness, or my inner yearning for God far more eloquently than any words of mine. So I adopted it as a language all of its own. And when I came to prayer exhausted, I would sometimes lie in this position and voice a simple prayer: 'Lord, there are no words to express what I long to say to you. Please interpret the language of my body lying prostrate before you.' At such times I would sense a strange warmth which I took to be the support, the strengthening or the cleansing of God.

I am glad, looking back, that no one made a video recording of my experimentations with bodily posture. To the observer, certain postures must look very comical. But I found that when my body, mind and spirit were co-ordinated, an air of expectancy pervaded my prayer and an alertness to God characterised my listening.

Sometimes I would stand as I came into God's presence

in the same way as many of the Old Testament prophets did.[3] At the same time, I would cup my hands, a gesture I use to show God that I am ready to receive whatever he wants to say or give to me. Sometimes I would tremble with anticipation as my body and my spirit waited attentively for a fresh visitation from God.

Usually, I would move from the standing position to kneeling. Sister Stella Mary had introduced me to the value of a prayer stool, an oblong stool nineteen centimetres high and eighteen centimetres wide which, when placed across the calves, supports the body, prevents the body's weight from cutting off the blood supply to the legs, and therefore enables a person to kneel for long periods in comparative comfort. A member of our congregation made a portable prayer stool for me, a gift I still value.

And my hands played an increasingly important part in my prayer. Sometimes I would hold them in my lap, palms upturned, a gesture of receptivity indicating that I was ready to receive anything God wanted to give me. At other times, as I knelt, I would bring my arms parallel to my body, spreading them out and tilting my palms very slightly as I turned them towards the front. Using this posture, my body says to God: 'I am your listening servant. I am yours. What is your will for me?'

When a sense of unworthiness swept over me, I would frequently fold my arms across my chest. And like Job and the Psalmist, I began to experiment with expressing praise and adoration to God, not simply with words, but by raising my hands and arms.[4] Occasionally, I would dance to some of the worship choruses I was growing to appreciate.

Gradually, I discovered that, in my body, I possessed an ally; a part of me which responded to the word of God's Spirit with greater ease than my mind; an ally who seemed able to assist the Holy Spirit in his work of revealing God's truth to my innermost being. There were times, which increased as the years fled by, when I would be still before God; I would stand or kneel, and stretch out my hands to receive from him whatever he wanted to give me; and, with my body receptive, an awareness of the presence of the living God would overwhelm me. In the stillness, I *knew* with my body, my mind and spirit that he *is* God. This convinced me early on that I must not ignore my body or neglect it, but rather must view it as an essential part of listening prayer, a part of me God created for his glory.[5]

Distractions

Even though my place of prayer was prepared and I had carved out a chunk of the day for listening to God, and even though I was training my body to co-operate rather than distract in this art form of prayer, it would frequently happen that as soon as I closed the prayer room door and settled down on my prayer stool my mind would buzz with noise. What would happen day after day is that I would remember that there was no bread in the bread-bin or that there were no eggs in the fridge, or stillness would be the time when I would remember certain letters which really should be written, or phone calls which should have been made.

Distractions of other kinds crowded in on me too. There was the blue-tit which sat on the window-sill of my prayer room while I prayed, and knocked on the window with his beak. And there were the pigeons which perched on the sloping roof and cooed gently but persistently while I tried to focus on God. At first both these internal and external distractions irritated me. I felt guilty, too, fearing that my progress in listening to God must be painfully slow if I could be side-tracked by such trivia.

But James Borst seemed to take such intrusions for granted. Robert Llewellyn, too, assumed that the Christian called to contemplate would encounter such difficulties. Both gave practical suggestions which helped me leap this hurdle.

Robert Llewellyn suggested that when we pray we imagine that we are rather like motor launches. Coming downstream float flotsam and jetsam of every kind. We are to keep our eyes on the goal, Jesus, and simply allow all this paraphernalia to pass us by. Meanwhile, we push our way through it, steadfastly heading for our destination: God and attentiveness to him.

I enjoyed taking authority over disrupting noises in this way. I would keep a piece of paper and a pen beside me. If I remembered some shopping which needed to be done urgently I would jot down the necessary items and return to the work of listening. When other thoughts vied for attention, I would steer my way through them, as Robert Llewellyn suggested. As for the blue-tit, the pigeons and the occasional troublesome motor-bike roaring past the house, I learned to *use* these sounds; I learned to translate them into prayer rather than to fight them as though they were enemies of God. I would hear the blue-tit's beak tap against the window and simply say: 'Thank you, Lord, for being nearer to me than that blue-tit; for your love which is more persistent than the sound of his hammering.' I would return to prayer and the noise would disappear, not because it had stopped, but because it had been dealt with, leaving me free to listen.

As I phased in and out of prayer like this, the name Jesus was often on my lips. I was not using the Lord's name as a mantra. Rather I used it as a reminder of my goal in prayer: to encounter the living God, to be met by him, held by him, commune with him and hear him. Somehow it seemed natural, therefore, to call him by name. As I come to prayer today, I still repeat that name often. And if my concentration is broken for any reason, I return to the stillness by repeating that name slowly and silently. While I do this, I find that my breathing deepens automatically. James Borst suggests that these two methods – using a word of love, like the name Jesus, and consciously breathing more deeply – bring us back from the siding into which distractions shunt us, and on to the main track of prayer. I find this a helpful concept, one which I still use.

Phasing-in to stillness

John Donne used a memorable phrase to describe the prelude to prayer: 'To tune the instrument at the gate'. Both James Borst and Robert Llewellyn emphasised the need for a phasing-in period: a few moments when we can re-focus from the concerns of the day, relax and open ourselves to attentiveness to the Spirit of God which is contemplation.

I found in the early days of exploration into stillness that I needed this re-orientation phase. I still need it.

Sometimes I would delay shutting the prayer room door quite deliberately. Instead, I would tidy the house while I composed myself and prayed a mental prayer: 'Lord, quieten my mind and my heart as I prepare for this time with you.' Sometimes I would go to my prayer room immediately my time for prayer came round. There I kept a tall, fat, red candle and I used to light this whenever I came to pray. It held no theological significance for me, only a practical one. If my mind was spinning like a top, as often it does, I would watch the flame flicker, listen to the wick splutter and spit, take careful note of the poker-still body and ask God to bring *me* into that kind of alive stillness.

The focal point of my prayer room was a cross. During this prelude to prayer, I would sometimes simply kneel at the foot of that cross and gaze at it. The cross of Jesus, that compelling symbol of sacrificial love, challenges me to centre my thoughts, not on *my* needs, *my* worries, *my* fears, *my* wants, but on Jesus. And as I gazed, I would find that in the wordlessness of silent wonder Jesus would emerge from the background of my mind and become the principal character in this drama of listening prayer.

Occasionally, as I phased into stillness, I would resort to a method of prayer made famous by one of the mystics. In my prayer room, in addition to the candle and the cross, I had a chair, an old wicker-work one painted white. Particularly if I came to prayer exhausted or hurting for some reason, I would imagine Jesus sitting in this chair. I would lay my head on the cushion, as though it were his lap, and weep or sigh or 'just be' in his felt presence. This kind of preliminary to prayer was therapy; on many occasions it infused my whole being with a sense of God's healing and peace; it was a form of listening which defies definition.

Preparing to listen

More and more, meditative music helped me to drop into the inner stillness which, for me, became the pre-requisite for alert, attentive and accurate listening to God. Almost always I would refer to the notes I had taken from James Borst's booklet and make my own response to them:

> Just sit down and relax. Slowly and deliberately let all tension flow away, and gently seek an awareness of the immediate and personal presence of God... You can relax and let go of everything, precisely *because* God is present. In his presence nothing really matters; all things are in his hands. Tension, anxiety, worry, frustration all melt away before him, as snow before the sun.
>
> Seek peace and inner silence. Let your mind, heart, will and feelings become tranquil and serene. Let inner storms subside: obsessional thoughts, passionate desires of will and emotions. 'Seek peace and follow after it' (Ps. 34:14).[6]

If I was still conscious of tension, I would tighten every muscle in my body quite deliberately. Then, starting with the facial muscles, I would relax them. At the same time, I would ask God to spread his life and his energy through me. And almost always I became aware that I was being impregnated by God's peace.

In this way, I began to serve my apprenticeship in the art of. listening to God. Increasingly, I came to value the simple techniques I have mentioned: a quiet, private place, a fixed time, the language of my body, dealing with distractions and the relaxation which enables the personality to unfold in the warm rays of the felt love of God. I still value them and find them essential, though, with the years, the emphasis I place on them has changed.

For me, learning to listen to God in this way has been rather like learning to drive a car. When I was a learner driver, between lessons I used to rehearse mentally the process of changing gear and think carefully about the technique of the three-point turn. In time, with experience, these procedures became almost automatic and required little thought.

Similarly, the prayer techniques I have described became a regular part of my routine. This did not result in complacency, however. I was always greedy for more. I say this with no sense of pride. With the realisation that prayer is a gift of God came the awareness that even the desire to pray had been engrafted by God himself. No one could work himself up to want to meet God in the way I thirsted for his presence at that time. It was a pure and precious gift.

Why was God enriching my life in this way? Why was prayer becoming such a profound experience? I was no super-saint, just an ordinary Christian leading an ordinary life, trying to be a good wife, a good mother and an effective witness for God in my neighbourhood.

For months no answer to that question was given, so I pressed on, growing all the time in my appreciation of silence, solitude and stillness before God. With the art of stillness came a greater ability to hear God. Phillip Keller has described the situation well:

It is within this inner stillness, within this utter

quietness, within this sweet solitude, that the Spirit of
the living God speaks most clearly to our spirits. It is
there, alone with him, that he makes himself real to us.
It is there we 'see' him most acutely with the inner eyes
of our awakened conscience. It is there he communes
with us calmly through the inner awareness of his
presence, speaking to us with ever-deepening conviction by his own wondrous word.[7]

This was becoming my experience. It filled me with
awe. At the time there were few people I could confide in
about this pilgrimage in the Spirit. That seemed
unimportant. What was more important was that I pursue
this purposeful prayer. Perhaps the time to talk would
come later.

Chapter 5
Preparing to Contemplate

Contemplative prayer was to be a rich source of listening to God. Day by day I would sit or stand or kneel in my prayer room, relax, allow tensions to slide away, focus on God, and a miracle would happen. As I closed my eyes to shut out visual stimuli, and as I closed my ears, as it were, by dealing authoritatively with the distractions which threatened my ability to tune in to God, it was as though, on the one hand, I closed a series of shutters on the surface level of my life, thus holding at bay hindrances to hearing the still, small voice of God, and on the other hand, I released a trigger which gave deeper, inner, hidden parts of myself permission to spark to life. As I attempted to focus, deliberately and unashamedly, on the presence of Christ, I would sometimes detect an inner stirring as though secret antennae were being aroused and alerted to pick up any and every signal the indwelling royal guest might choose to give.

This attentiveness, alertness and sense of anticipation was not unlike the in-tuneness I experienced when my children were babies. I would be cooking or gardening, reading or even sleeping, yet at the same time I would be alert to their feelings: their pleasure, their glee, their discomfort, their pain. Just as I had wanted, as a young mother, to be responsive to my offspring, so now I longed to respond to God in this intuitive way.

But there was so much more to learn. I loved the learning process. My highway code, which stayed with me almost always in the early days, was James Borst's booklet, *A Method of Contemplative Prayer*. At first I scarcely ever veered from this step-by-step guide to attentive stillness. Eventually, as I grew in confidence and experience, inevitably I developed methods of my own in my pursuit to refine the art form of listening to God. Each person who seeks to stand before the living God will discover his own way of doing so. This must happen. The secret of true prayer is to place oneself utterly and completely at the disposal of God's Spirit. Sometimes the Spirit might cause us to dance or to jump for joy; at other times the same Spirit might draw us into the depths of silence where all is too mysterious for words. Even so, while remaining flexible and responsive to the wind of the Spirit, there is value in being aware of formulae used by others which one can then adapt in one's own time and way. James Borst's formula was the launching pad which thrust me into orbit.

James Borst suggests that there are certain phases which the person eager to reach the presence of God either passes through or dwells in during the course of any one period of prayer. He suggests that, in contemplative prayer, there are nine such phases. Some of these are preparatory phases, one is the contemplative phase itself, then there is the afterglow. The person at prayer might move from one phase to the next during their hour of prayer. Alternatively, depending on circumstances or personal needs, the one praying might stay in one phase only on a particular occasion if that seems most helpful. The contemplative phase will not necessarily be reached during every prayer time.

Phase of relaxation and silence

The first phase, I found, was indispensable. This is the one I have already described where, deliberately, I relax and let go of everything: tension, worry, anxiety, frustration. It is the period of prayer when I attempt to obey God's commands given through the psalmist: 'Be still, and know that I am God' (Ps. 46:10).

James Borst suggests that, if necessary, the whole of one's prayer time should be devoted to this activity. I soon saw the reason for this suggestion. Until our bodies, minds and spirits let go of the clutter we bring to our places of prayer, we automatically tune out the still, small voice of God. Unless we come into stillness before God we do not detect either the fullness of his presence or the winsomeness of his voice.

This phase of prayer has a value all its own. As we stop struggling before God we make it possible for him to impregnate us with his Spirit. During this prelude to prayer I would sometimes imagine myself as a meadow being saturated and refreshed by a gentle fall of dew. At other times I would think of myself as a tree; I would feel the sap surge through my roots and the sun shine on my leaves and I would know myself nourished by God. Sometimes, during this initial phase of prayer, I would picture myself as a rock on the seashore and I would enjoy the warmth of the sun of God's love and the washing of the water of his Spirit lapping over me. At such times I felt cherished by God.

Phase of awareness of his presence

I found that unless I took the trouble to unwind in God's presence in this way, I failed to appreciate the next phase of prayer: the few minutes when I opened myself to an awareness of God's presence, attentiveness and care. And it was this part of prayer which was revolutionising my life, so it was worthwhile spending time to prepare for it.

I am not conscious that anyone had ever suggested to me that, having relaxed in the presence of God, I should take time to recollect that he dwells at the core of my being; that as my Father he is as attentive to my cry as a mother to the slightest whimper of her new-born baby; that his gaze is focused on me as eagerly and devotedly as a father fixes his love on his new-born child. But as I began to spend time in recognising that God delights in me in this way, that he desires intimacy with me more than I long for oneness with him, I was filled with a profound sense of security.

I think, for example, of an occasion when I was suffering from an acute sense of loneliness. As I entered my prayer room, removed my shoes, relaxed, and concentrated, not on the growing emptiness within, but on the presence of God, I seemed to see myself as fragile, helpless and vulnerable as a new-born baby. But I was not lying alone, unloved. No. The arms of God were cradling me, his finger was stroking my cheek, his eyes were twinkling down at me. I felt loved.

I could have read those consoling words, 'Underneath are the everlasting arms', (Deut. 33:27), and I could have meditated on God's promise, 'I have loved you with an everlasting love', (Jer. 31:3), but to see those arms and to experience that love caused the assurance in my head to trickle into my heart and to lodge there. It is one of the rich dividends of contemplative prayer, I find, that in the stillness familiar truths make an impact on my experience in a way which is healing, consoling or challenging.

Phase of surrender

The more practised I became in finding the still point before God where I could taste his love and feel his warmth, the more I longed to surrender every part of my being to him. I wanted to be able to make the claim Paul once made: 'I no longer live, but Christ lives in me' (Gal. 2:20). I wanted to move from my prayer room into my corner of the world 'pregnant with Christ', to borrow Catherine de Hueck Doherty's phrase. And so, most days, I would make a conscious attempt to hand back to God all that I am, all that I possess, all that I do and all that I feel: my counselling, my teaching, my writing; my personality, my sexuality, my love, my friendships; my home, my pain if I am hurting, my successes or failures. I would echo the prayer James Borst uses: 'Take me and all I have, and do with me whatever you will. Send me where you will. Use me as you will. I surrender myself and all I possess absolutely and entirely, unconditionally and forever, to your control.'[1]

Whenever I paused to think seriously about this far-reaching prayer and could pray it with integrity, I would notice the level of joy and love for God rise measurably inside me. My heart would burn with love for God. My ability and desire to make sacrifices for him increased. This is hardly surprising. As Thomas Merton once put it, 'The deepest prayer at its nub is a perpetual surrender to God'.[2]

As I pray with others from time to time, I notice that there seems to be a law which links the awareness of God's presence with surrender to him. I think of an occasion when I was praying with a close friend of mine. He had asked me to pray for him that the parched places of his life might be revitalised by the life-giving waters of the Spirit of God. That night God met him in a most moving way. On a subsequent occasion, sensing that the Holy Spirit was leading him along the route I had travelled, the path of contemplative prayer, we again opened ourselves to receive whatever God wanted to give us. Then we kept total silence for several minutes.

It was my friend who broke the silence temporarily: 'I feel light-headed,' he admitted, 'and my heart is pounding.' The sense of the presence of God filled my study where we were praying. 'I believe these sensations are the Spirit's work,' I suggested. 'Let's just remain silent and open to him.' After several more minutes of complete silence, my friend, a young man who is not given to sentimentality or emotionalism, slumped back in his chair and sighed: 'I love him. I really love him. I could sing the chorus, "I love you Lord," right now, and really mean it.'

He said no more. There was no need. I could see on his face the look of longing love he felt for Jesus at that moment as he contemplated him. It did not surprise me that, from time to time after this overwhelming of the Spirit of God, this young man talked to me about offering himself to God for full-time service. The awareness of God's presence and the surrender of all our faculties belong together. If they do not, prayer can simply degenerate into self-indulgence.

Phase of acceptance

The fourth phase of prayer recommended by James Borst almost always causes me discomfort, to the same extent as the first few phases bring the overwhelming of the Spirit's presence. This is the time when we invite God to put his finger on specific situations, sins or attitudes which would block our ability to listen to God.

Jesus reminded us that part of the Holy Spirit's mission in life is to convict us of sin, to cross-examine us until we admit our failure. The further I progressed on this path of listening prayer, the more ruthless God seemed to become in highlighting inconsistencies in my life, showing me where he required me to change. At times I rebelled. At other times I squealed. God's demands are absolute, uncompromising. When he exposed sin I knew there would be no peace in prayer until I had played my part and obeyed his command to renounce it.

I think, for example, of an occasion when my husband and I had quarrelled. I made no attempt to hide my anger and bitterness from God. And he made no attempt to hide his requirement from me.

> 'Forgive David,' he said. 'Go and apologise.'
> 'But, Lord, it was *his* fault, not mine,' I protested.
> 'Never mind. You make the peace,' came the un-compromising reply.

On another occasion, as I gave God the opportunity to

highlight areas of my life which he wanted to change, the dislike of a member of our congregation rose to the surface of my mind. The degree of irritability I encountered shocked me. This realisation drew from me a prayer: 'Lord, give me *your* love for her.' As though in answer to that prayer, I became aware of this girl's suffering. God seemed to pour into my receptive heart a great compassion for her, the compassion which is identification with another's pain and the desire, where possible, to alleviate that person's loneliness.

I still find this phase of prayer by far the most disconcerting. It is the part of prayer I most frequently omit. And my life is impoverished because of it. I recognise why I avoid this listening. One reason is that I am afraid: afraid of the sacrifices which may be demanded of me. Another reason is that, so often in my listening prayer, I am more concerned to receive the consolations of God than the God of consolations, the one who sets out to show me the truth about himself and the truth about myself, the one whose mission is to change me into his likeness.

Phase of repentance and forgiveness

Thomas Merton claims that 'to pray means to change'. He adds: 'Prayer if it is real is an acknowledgement of ... our open-ness to be changed.'[3] Whenever I gave God the opportunity to show me myself and the areas of life which he wanted to prune or purge, I passed, with thankfulness, into the fifth phase of prayer. This is the place where James Borst urges the would-be contemplative to be ruthlessly honest: 'We face God as we are: sinful, spiritually handicapped and disabled in many ways, chronic patients. And we accept these handicaps and disabilities because he accepts us as we are and because he loves us as we are.'[4] James Borst is not suggesting that we become complacent about the sin which soils our lives. On the contrary, his challenge to cast it at the foot of the cross is compelling. But for me, the startling part of this

phase of prayer is his insistence that we not only confess
but *receive* forgiveness.

The introvert, particularly if that person comes from an
evangelical background, is good at confessing and
notoriously bad at receiving forgiveness. I am an introvert
and an evangelical. These words never cease to amaze me
even though I have been reading them for nine years.

> We are not permitted to nurse a sense of guilt: we must
> fully and completely accept and embrace his forgiveness
> and love. Guilt feeling and inferiority feeling before
> God are expressions of selfishness, of self-centredness:
> we give greater importance to our little sinful self than
> to his immense and never-ending love. We must
> surrender our guilt and our inferiority to him; *his
> goodness is greater than our badness. We must accept
> his joy in loving and forgiving us.* It is a healing grace to
> surrender our sinfulness to his mercy.[5]

'His goodness is greater than our badness.'
'We must accept his joy in forgiving us.'
I recorded in my prayer journal an occasion when God
wormed these words into my realisation. My emotions
were in turmoil at the time. The problem was that I was
working with a male colleague whose warmth and
gentleness, tenderness and spirituality I was growing to
appreciate. He was eliciting from me a response which
was equally warm and this resulted in a special closeness
which seemed like a gift from God.

Whenever God entrusts us with something of value and
beauty, Satan sets himself the task of destroying or
distorting it. In this instance he tried to soil this friendship
by bombarding my mind with day-dreams and suggestions, thoughts and fantasies which, if translated into
practice would turn *philia*, warm, compassionate, tender
love into *eros*, a romantic love which would threaten my
marriage and my integrity as a person.

At first, knowing that there is a close correlation between spiritual closeness and sexual awakening, I resisted each temptation firmly. A civil war raged inside but I fought to win. But gradually, my efforts weakened and I surrended my imagination to the impure pictures which flashed frequently on the screen of my mind. While masquerading as a God-pleasing person, this poison was polluting me. Consequently, the reservoir of prayer dwindled to a mere puddle. The yearning to listen to God waned. And peace evaporated.

God disciplines those he loves. And he disciplined me. It was while I was sitting in church one Sunday morning that his voice reached me through the tangle of my emotions. 'You've lost your cutting edge', was all he said. And I knew that he was correct.

A deep, dark sadness crept over me as I reflected on this home-truth. 'What do I do, Lord?' I whispered. My answer came through the sermon. 'If you have lost your effectiveness for God because you have been sinning, admit it, acknowledge your failure and apply the blood of Jesus to the stain so that you may be forgiven.'

Later that day, I sat in the garden with my prayer journal and did just that. In a letter to God I poured out my repentance. When I had finished writing, I paused to listen. Into my mind came a picture of a pair of hands holding a piece of white fabric which was soiled and stained. I sensed the hands were God's hands and the piece of fabric represented my sin-spoiled life. As I watched, the hands held the fabric into a vat containing liquid. After several minutes, they gathered up the length of cloth and lifted it from the detergent. The stain had disappeared. The material was whiter than it had ever been. And God's voice seemed to whisper: 'My blood, shed for you, is the best detergent in the world.' I was so deeply moved that I wept tears of gratitude. I was so amazed at this sheer, undeserved goodness that I felt numb for several hours. I was so overwhelmed that I recorded the awe in my prayer journal. I was responding to the verse which claims that when God forgives, there is 'nothing left against you.' And I wrote:

'Lord, I can scarcely drink in this good news. Can it be true that you have wiped the slate clean of *all* the sin of the past few months? Yes! With my mind I know it. May that word NOTHING echo through the labyrinths of my entire being. NO THING. Not one single thought. No fantasy. No lust. NOTHING! Zero! The score against me from the divine perspective is nought. What relief! What joy! I am free: free from the guilt, free from the stain, free from the power of the Evil One, free to say no to all his fiendish suggestions. For this miracle, my Lord and Master, my Saviour, I praise you. May I be a faithful steward of the mystery of this grace of forgiveness. May I be a faithful steward, too, of *your* gift of love.

God's forgiveness and love cannot be earned. It is always undeserved. Nevertheless it is to be received with humbleness and brokenness of spirit. It is to be relished. It is to be accepted with thanksgiving. It reflects the victory Jesus won at Calvary. It turns our disgrace into trophies of his grace.

Listening prayer, I was discovering, operates when we are in the pits, needing to be rescued by God, and it is operative, too, when we soar to unexpected spiritual peaks. And, of course, God goes on speaking in the ordinary, in-between days when life seems mundane, even monotonous. He not only speaks, he woos us, calling us to receive him into our lives, persuading us to fix our gaze on him.

Chapter 6
Continuing to Contemplate

I preached at a friend's wedding just before I began to write this chapter. After the ceremony, the bride and groom invited those who had taken part in the service to congregate on the steps of the church to be photographed. The group formed: the bride, the groom, the vicar of the church, a friend who had officiated at the service, the two people who had read Bible passages, a young man who had sung a solo, and me. We smiled – and shivered, because it was a cold, grey day. One photograph was taken and we began to move away. But the photographer cried out: 'Hold it! I want to take another one just like that.'

'Hold it!' Perhaps that is the simplest and most accurate definition of contemplative prayer: the deepest, most mysterious method of listening to God which I know of.

In the last chapter, I described the way I went about preparing to contemplate. The phases of prayer are rather like pieces of a jig-saw puzzle. When you fit them together, you realise that God has been preparing you for the moment when you 'hold it'; when your heart and mind and will are relaxed, focused on him, surrendered to him, cleansed and renewed so that you are ready to gaze on him in adoring love and to know yourself the object of his undivided affection and attention.

Archbishop Anthony Bloom captures the nuances of this dimension of listening prayer with a simple story of a peasant who had formed the habit of slipping into a certain church at a certain time of day with clockwork regularity. There, day by day, he would sit and, apparently, do nothing. The parish priest observed this regular, silent visitor. One day, unable to contain his curiosity any longer, he asked the old man why he came to the church, alone, day in, day out. Why waste his time in this way?

The old man looked at the priest and with a loving twinkle in his eye gave this explanation: 'I look at him. He looks at me. And we tell each other that we love each other.'

This is contemplation in a nutshell. This is the essence of listening prayer. Though I was a mere beginner, and still consider myself to be no more than a novice, this was the gift God was giving me. This was the reason why I carved out a whole hour a day to abandon myself to the stillness in which the love of Christ could be felt. This was why I was at pains to use the phases I have described to opt out of the crazy whirlpool of ceaseless activity into which I am so quickly sucked and to reach the calmer waters of the prayer of silence. Phillip Keller captures the benefits of this stillness well:

For the man or woman who has come to know and love the Lord God in the depths of such intimacy, the times of solitude are the most precious in all of life. They are a rendezvous with the Beloved. They are anticipated with eagerness. They are awaited with expectancy . . . For the person who has found in God a truly loving heavenly Father, gentle interludes with him alone are highlights of life. For the one who has found Christ the dearest friend among all the children of earth, quiet times in his company are the oases of life. For the individual conscious of the comradeship of God's gracious Spirit in the stillness of solitude, these intervals are the elixir of life.[1]

Such was my experience. Indeed, such *is* my experience. No words of mine can hope to do justice to the encounter with God which takes place in such silence. It is as hard to recapture with a pen as it is to describe the scene outside the cottage window which I have been gazing at for the past five minutes. I can tell you that raindrops glisten as they hang like pearls from the rose bush which almost touches my window pane; that the fronds of the weeping willow are waving to the cars which wind their way along the valley; that a blackbird is surveying the moors as he sits on the telephone wire and sings; that the sun is trying to shine on the rain-drenched hills. I can describe the colours: the purple aubrietia cascading over my neighbour's grey stone walls, the yellow pansies in her garden, the coral pink of her rhododendron bushes, the scarlet of her tulips, and the variegated virgin greens which cover the countryside in spring. But this is only a fragment of the scene which delights me. You cannot hear the thrush trilling nor hear the chaffinches chattering nor see the buds bursting with life, nor feel the creative energy of the countryside in May. If you would appreciate the full extent of the beauty before me you must witness the glory of this place for yourself.

Similarly, the wonders of contemplation can be appreciated only by those who contemplate, for as Stephen Verney, the Bishop of Repton, rightly says, 'contemplation is an opening of the eyes...'[2] It is losing oneself in what one sees and hears in the same way as one loses oneself in a spectacular sunrise or a magnificent view from an aeroplane.

Stephen Verney suggests that there are three stages of contemplation: first, 'it is me and him'. I come to prayer conscious of myself, my need, my desires. I pour these out to God. Second, prayer becomes 'him and me'. Gradually, I become more conscious of the presence of God than of myself. 'Then it is only him.'[3] God's presence arrests me, captivates me, warms me, works on me. It is mystery, reality, certainty – awesome. As an unknown author of the thirteenth century put it: 'While you are quiet and exist in a calm and simple awareness of his presence, your heart seeks him out and opens to receive his love. It is a prayer which is wordless, fed by a quiet ardor.'[4] Or, as another contemplative has struggled to express the inexpressible:

> You turn yourself entirely to his presence. You steadily look at him. His presence becomes more real to you. He holds your inward sight. Your glance simply and lovingly rests on him. Your prayer is nothing but a loving awareness of him: I look because I love; I look in order to love, and my love is fed and influenced by looking ...[5]

What does the contemplative see when he gazes in this way? I cannot speak for anyone else. I can speak for myself. For me, the seeing varies from day to day.

In the early days I would often dwell on the vision of Christ contained in the Book of Revelation. As I contemplated, I would catch my breath as a hint of the glory of the wounded, wondrous, much-worshipped Lamb of God would impress itself on me:

> Then I looked and heard the voice of many angels, numbering thousands upon thousands, and ten thousand times ten thousand. They encircled the throne and the living creatures and the elders. In a loud voice they sang:
>
> > Worthy is the Lamb, who was slain,
> > to receive power and wealth and wisdom and strength
> > and honour and glory and praise!
>
> Then I heard every creature in heaven and on earth and under the earth and on the sea, and all that is in them, singing:

To him who sits on the throne and to the Lamb
be praise and honour and glory and power, for ever
and ever!

The four living creatures said, 'Amen', and the elders
fell down and worshipped (Rev. 5:11–14).

In the early days, too, while the cross was the visual
focus in my prayer room, the sufferings of Christ,
physical, emotional and psychological, would often fill
my horizon as I fixed my attention on love crucified.

Since my visit to Israel, where the aliveness of Jesus
struck me with fresh force, and where a bronze statue of the
Lord leaping with resurrection joy made a deep impression on me, often, as I kneel or stand or sit in an
attitude of listening prayer, God's strength, vitality,
power, authority and even sense of fun overwhelm me and
intermingle with the pain and glory I have already
mentioned.

This morning, for example, God delighted me with the
reminder of the *joie de vivre* which is an expression of the
abundant life Jesus enjoyed as well as promised to others.
As I focused my attention on God, C. S. Lewis' vigorous
account of the resurrection flooded back into my mind. In
his children's fantasy, *The Lion, the Witch and the
Wardrobe*, Aslan, the lion, who represents Jesus, was
sacrificed and then mysteriously brought back to life:

'Oh children,' said the Lion, 'I feel my strength coming
back to me. Oh children, catch me if you can!' He stood
for a second, his eyes very bright, his limbs quivering,
lashing himself with his tail. Then he made a leap, high
over their heads, and landed on the other side of the
table. Laughing, though she didn't know why, Lucy
scrambled over it to reach him. Aslan leaped again. A
mad chase began. Round and round the hill-top he led
them, now hopelessly out of their reach, now tossing

them in the air with his huge and beautifully velveted
paws and catching them again, and now stopping
unexpectedly so that all three of them rolled over
together in a happy laughing heap of fur and arms and
legs.[6]

I could never predict beforehand what the result of the
listening would be. Nor could I anticipate how long the
sense of the awareness of God's presence would last.
Usually, I find the moments of acute in-touchness with
God are fleeting, but real. I soon discovered that I must be
content with what God gave, enjoy it and benefit from it
without trying to cling or crave for more. He might choose
to reveal himself momentarily, he might linger. That is
his responsibility. Mine is simply to be ready.

Phase of receiving

And I wanted to be ready always. As bulbs in spring stretch
their green fingers upwards in response to the warm rays
of the sun, so I was responding to the felt, experienced
presence of God. And I discovered that the phase of
contemplation is not the final phase of prayer. There is an
afterglow to be enjoyed. The first phase after the moment
of contemplation is the phase of receiving. As James Borst
puts it, '"Seek and you will always find" becomes "Seek
and you will always be found."'[7]

Having spent years in prayer asking God for things, this
phase of the afterglow was sheer delight. At first I scarcely
dared to believe James Borst's claim:

'He responds: He turns to me. He seeks me. He is
anxious to invade my spirit. He wants that his Spirit
possess me. I bask in the warmth of his love. I feel his
gaze upon me. Jesus, my Lord, is eager to possess my
heart with which to love his Father, and with which to
radiate his love ... His presence brings a deep spiritual
peace, a share in his 'sabbath' rest, a greater serenity,

ability to accept and to suffer, a lifting of despair, a welling up of joy and love, a floodlight, a strong desire to praise and thank him.'[8]

But these claims became true to my experience.

Eighteen months after my initiation into this life of listening prayer, I began to keep a prayer journal where I recorded some of the things I wanted to express to God as well as some of his responses. In the autumn of 1978 I wrote:

I find prayer exciting because I never know in advance how God is going to meet with me. The Divine Lover sometimes comes as the Father, the one who is saving the best robe for the worst child, the Father who gave his own Son, such is the generosity of his loving. Sometimes my Lord comes as the loving, searching Shepherd, sometimes as life. Sometimes as energy.

I recorded the sense of awe which overwhelmed me with every realisation that it is *God* who takes the initiative in this kind of prayer:

My knowledge of God is becoming deeper. It is far less an intellectual knowing and progressing towards the intimate knowing experienced by a husband and wife: union. Sometimes he comes to me as the Bridegroom to his Bride and in that knowing there is such awesome love. As I write that now, it seems too wonderful that Almighty God – the generous one – should meet *me* in that way and yet that is part of his generosity that it is he who takes the initiative.

All my life, the teaching I had received on prayer had placed the responsibility for my relationship with God firmly on my shoulders. I had been taught to seek God: in his Word, in church, in the fellowship. Even when I had

had a conversion experience at the age of seventeen, the emphasis seemed to focus on *my* commitment: it was *me* giving *my* life to God. But now the emphasis had changed. God seemed to underline the true situation: that the initiative in the prayer of listening was not mine but his. The initiative of love, similarly, was not mine, but his. As Thomas Merton puts it: 'True contemplation is not a psychological trick but a theological grace. It can come to us *only* as a gift.'[9] And as the author of *The Cloud of Unknowing* reminds us, '*He* kindled your desire for himself, and bound you to him by the chain of such longing.'[10]

These facts penned so poignantly by Stephen Verney stunned me into silent worship and wonder:

This is the nature of the encounter, not that I am stumbling towards the Abba Father, but that the Abba Father is running towards me. It is not that I love God but that God believes in me. The discovery at the heart of contemplation is not that I am contemplating the divine love, but that the divine love is contemplating me. He sees me and understands and accepts me, he has compassion on me, he creates me afresh from moment to moment, and he protects me and is with me through death and into life beyond.[11]

To know oneself loved, believed in, understood, accepted, trusted and constantly renewed by God is a humbling experience. At least, I found it so. And it took time for the realisation of these truths to trickle from my head into my heart. As, gradually, they lodged there, the phase of receiving began, not only to make sense to me but to become a priority.

Jesus now featured in the dialogue of prayer in a new way: not just by whispering into my ear but by acting on my behalf.

I think of the time when I wondered whether the

glandular fever germ would ever leave my body, when my body was weary and I was lonely. One day, as I prayed, I poured out my frustration to God. During the phase of receiving in prayer, I found myself re-enacting the parable of the Good Samaritan. But in the video which played through my imagination, I seemed to be the wounded person lying helpless on the deserted road. As I opened myself to receive from Jesus, he came to me displaying all the tenderness and skill attributed to the Good Samaritan. The encounter was so powerful that I could sense him anointing my emotional wounds, entering into my loneliness, picking me up and pouring into me the courage I needed to carry on.

A recurring picture which never ceased to amaze and comfort me also found its roots in one of Jesus's parables. I would picture myself as a forlorn lamb which had lost its way and lost its companions. While I was busy bleating or panicking or running round in small circles, I would see Jesus striding towards me. I would sometimes see his smile. I would sense his immense strength. Sometimes I would feel him put me on his shoulders and carry me back to the proper path. At other times he would simply stand and cuddle or chastise me.

Receiving God's love in this vivid way reinforced for me the reality of the God who is always there, the God who cares. It encouraged me to open myself to the surge of God's love and not to dictate to him how he might or might not express this love.

Phase of Praise and Thanksgiving

It also carried me across the threshold into another phase of prayer: the phase of praise and thanksgiving. From time to time God would challenge me to learn to receive life as a gift from himself instead of living life at such breakneck speed that there was no time to think thankfully.

As I responded to this challenge, I learned to savour the good gifts God sends: a perfect rose, the scent of honeysuckle, the embrace of a friend, the taste of bacon. As this savouring became a part of life, I would thank God for the gift of electricity when I used my cooker instead of taking modern technology for granted. And as I fell asleep at night, I would watch an action replay of the previous twenty-four hours in my mind and select particular people and events for which I wanted to praise God. At such times life became a symphony of praise.

As time went on, this heart-felt gratitude to God began to be expressed in a whole variety of ways. One morning, a few months after this journey into contemplative prayer had begun in earnest, having gazed at the features of the Lord I was learning to trust in a deeper, richer way than ever before, I took up my guitar and started to sing a song of praise to its accompaniment. After a few minutes I was playing a chord sequence I had not learned and singing a tune I had never heard before. The language I used was not English, but tongues, a method of praising God I had once considered weird and superfluous, but which I now value immensely.

But the times when I wondered whether my heart would burst with praise almost always happened at the convent which eventually became my spiritual home. At 9.0a.m. each morning, the sisters celebrate Holy Communion and I would join them for this highlight of the day's worship. Usually it was a simple, short service lasting not more than half an hour. There would be no music, just the liturgy, Bible readings, prayer and the sacrament – the bread and wine. At the close of the service, everyone would kneel in silent adoration of Jesus, the one who had fed us with these symbols of his body and blood. It was then, having been brought into silence, having been brought face to face with the mystery of God and having been fed by him, that praise would surge from somewhere deep inside of me and beg to be expressed: either in silent wonder, or in sighs and groans, or in a burst of song. The urge to sing was so strong sometimes that after Communion I would go to the bottom of the garden where no one could hear me and sing under the pine trees, or I would take my guitar to the garden shed and strum it and sing to God there. To be gripped by such praise was intoxicating, and I realised that very often I approach prayer, praise and thanksgiving from the wrong angle. I rush into God's presence, blurt out some superficial sentences of gratitude, but never pause to encounter him. When the encounter comes first, I realised, the level of praise is deepened, the experience more real.

Phase of Intercession

And I learned that having dropped into the stillness of God, contemplated him, received from him and given thanks for who he is and what he has done, I was ready to intercede for others. But the nature of intercession changed. The focus of the prayer was not the person for whom I was praying, as it had been in the past. No. The focus of my intercessory prayer was Jesus himself. This refocusing revolutionised my practice of interceding for others. The acute awareness of the presence of Jesus persuaded me that I need not fumble for fine words in order to present to Jesus the needs of others. All that was needed was that I should pass the person or situation into his all-knowing, all-wise, all-capable and all-caring hands.

The consciousness of Christ's presence changed my prayer for another reason also. Instead of dictating to God what he should do to alleviate a certain person's suffering or to sort out a complex crisis, I learned, as I held the situation to him, to listen for an answer to the question: 'Lord, is there anything you would like me to do for this person to show them that you are in control or that you care?' I found that God is faithful in responding to that sort of question and very often requires me to form a part of the answer to my own prayers.

There never seems to be enough time to complete such

intercession in my specific prayer time. Most of my interceding spills over into my day, so I lift people and circumstances to God while I am hoovering or walking or driving the car or resting after lunch. God hears. He acts. In this prayer we simply sidle alongside the great intercessor, Jesus himself, and enjoy the privilege of becoming his prayer partner.

I could never be certain from day to day which of these phases of prayer would occupy most of my prayer time. What I could be certain of was that my experience of God would leave me panting for more. St Bernard said of contemplative prayer: it is a 'searching never satisfied but without any restlessness'. And Gregory of Nyssa observed: 'The one who looks up to God never ceases in that desire.' In a small way I was beginning to testify to these twin feelings and I wanted to press on because more experienced prayers persuaded me that one of the rewards of this particular search is to go on searching.

Chapter 7
Back to the Bible

I was troubled. People in my church fellowship were becoming suspicious of my prayer pilgrimage. One girl put the anxiety of many others into words: 'I think you're going overboard. You're allowing those mystics to influence you too much. You're in danger of betraying your evangelical heritage.' Others refrained from expressing their ambivalence at the time but confessed to me later, 'We thought we'd lost you to silence for ever.'

I understood this fear. Nevertheless it hurt. It hurt because it seemed as though I was not trusted. And it hurt to hear mature Christians express so much criticism and suspicion of those whose experience of God was somewhat different from their own. Whenever unfair comments were made about Catholic spirituality, for example, tears would prick my eyes and I would catch myself crying inside.

I am not saying that it was inappropriate for my friends to question what I was doing. Neither am I saying that I could not see why they were doing it. Until this phase of my life, I, too, had been bitterly prejudiced against 'high church practices' and particularly against Catholicism. My father, a staunch Baptist, had refused so much as to buy a Christmas card with a candle on it because to him it smacked of being Catholic. Ingrained in me from childhood was the belief that no good thing could come from Rome. But now I was beginning to catch a glimpse of how misguided that prejudice was. I am not saying that I accepted everything Catholic spirituality stands for. Neither am I saying that it ever occurred to me to become a Roman Catholic or even a high Anglican. What I am saying is that the monks I met at Mount St Bernard Abbey challenged the hard crust of contempt which covered me, not by anything they said, but by the life they lived: particularly by the quality of their prayer. I could see for myself that these men had plumbed depths of prayer which no one from my spiritual tradition had ever shown me. And I wanted what they experienced. Moreover, I believed that God wanted it for me, that he had provided these nursery slopes of prayer for me. And I recognised early on in my quest that I did not have to buy the whole Catholic package in order to benefit from their experience of prayer. Neither is God bound by the confines of our denominations.

Even so, I was torn in two. My husband, I could tell, was worried about me. Occasionally we attempted to discuss my growing interest in silence, meditation and contemplative prayer. But our minds failed to meet. He was afraid that I was travelling up a cul-de-sac which would result only in disillusionment. I was afraid that he was trying to squeeze me into a spiritual mould from which I had been set free. 'What am I to do?' On the one hand I seem to be standing on the threshold of a dynamic dimension of prayer which is revolutionising my life and on the other hand I seem to be alarming a number of people, including my husband.' I put this kind of question to myself on several occasions and the absence of an answer left me even more confused. I recorded this confusion in my prayer journal on one occasion. Writing to God, I said:

I want to confess to you the confusion I feel over the whole area of prayer. I so long to follow your leading in this – into silence. But I see this creating a bigger and

bigger gulf between David and me... Father, I feel
resentment. Why have you led me this way? Why can't
he understand? I feel deep anger and sorrow that over
the years I have listened to and assented to untruths
about many of your children [meaning Roman
Catholics]. Yes, I want to be caught up in your work of
reconciliation. But it hurts and I sometimes feel so
alone...'

But I was troubled for another reason, too. Although I
sensed that God was giving me a priceless pearl in this gift
of prayer, I had been taught that I was to be a 'guardian of
the gospel' and to ensure that my philosophy of life and
my behaviour were always in alignment with the clear
teaching of scripture. So far, although I had been
fascinated and helped by the rhythm of prayer I dropped
into at Mount St Bernard Abbey, at Whitby, and now at
home, and although I was thrilled by the teaching on
prayer I was receiving from the books I have mentioned,
references to the Bible's teaching on listening to God were
only oblique. I could not say for certain that the belief that
God still speaks today is firmly rooted in scripture.

How can John Powell be sure that God is as available to
speak to us today as he was to speak to Abraham, Isaac,
Jacob and Jeremiah? How can James Borst be certain that
it is *God* who will manifest himself in stillness? How can I
decide whether the overwhelming spiritual experiences
originate in God?

These questions and others like them bothered me, not
only because I loved the Bible and was firmly committed to
live biblically, but also because I knew that many Bible-
believing scholars pour scorn on voices and experiences.
In the circles in which I lived and worked the counter-
claim prevailed: that God has spoken through his Son and
through his revealed Word, the Bible. Since this revelation
contains everything we need 'for teaching, rebuking
correcting and training in righteousness' (2 Tim. 3:16),

God has no more need to speak.

Jim Packer describes this viewpoint powerfully and more generously than many:

> While it is not for us to forbid God to reveal things apart from scripture, or to do anything else (he is God, after all!), we may properly insist that the New Testament discourages Christians from expecting to receive God's words to them by any other channel than that of attentive application to themselves of what is given to us twentieth-century Christians in holy scripture.[1]

Trapped between this teaching, the anxiety of my friends and an irresistible thirst to know more about listening to God, there seemed only one way forward. I would have to search the Bible for myself to see whether it describes the kind of listening to God which had struck a chord within my heart.

'I'll do my own research. I'll comb the scriptures and apply to them three questions: Does the Bible address itself to the subject of listening to God? If so, what exactly does it say? How did God speak to men and women in the days when the Bible was written?'

Having made this resolve, I determined to be as thorough as possible. I raided my husband's study and collected every version of the Bible I could find, gathered together a stack of Bible commentaries, unearthed the fat, red New Bible Commentary I had used in student days, treated myself to a brand new Concordance and re-organised my own study to accommodate the booklets and articles and books on prayer which had helped me in some way. Thus surrounded by studies of prayer written by teachers of prayer and people of prayer from a variety of Christian traditions, I began my own quest into the Bible's teaching on listening to God.

God's promises

One of the first passages of the Bible I turned to intrigued me. It was the familiar passage from the fourth gospel: 'I am the good shepherd; I know my sheep and my sheep know me... I have other sheep that are not of this sheep pen. I must bring them also. *They too will listen to my voice*, and there shall be one flock and one shepherd' (John 10:14-16, italics mine). Two sentences from this passage gripped me. First, Jesus's claim to be 'the Good Shepherd'. Second, his promise. 'They too will listen to my voice.'

I began to tease out what might have been in Jesus's mind when he described himself as the Good Shepherd, a pen-picture which does not necessarily communicate itself accurately to the Western reader.

As I meditated on these words: 'Good Shepherd', my mind flew first to Greece where we had travelled on one occasion. I remembered commenting to my husband as we drove through mile upon mile of arid countryside: 'Have you noticed that you never see sheep here without an accompanying shepherd? At home it's the exact opposite. You scarcely ever see a shepherd, just fields full of unaccompanied sheep.'

My mind wandered from Greece to Israel. Tired of the heat and narrow streets thronging with tourists, my husband and I wandered out of Nazareth to picnic on a grassy slope we could see in the distance. There we met a youth carrying a new-born lamb, a shepherd boy.

He showed us his lamb with obvious pride. 'It's mine. It's not quite twenty-four hours old.' He also pointed to the other sheep grazing peacefully in the long grass. This boy was in charge of seventeen sheep including the baby lamb. Each sheep had a name. Each responded to that name. When the shepherd called, they followed. His relationship with these sheep, which belonged to his father, was intimate. He treated them not as possessions, but as persons. So he whispered in the lamb's woolly ear in the same way as a mother would coo over her baby. He told his little flock his news as they walked from pasture to pasture. He chided them when they wandered away from him or when they strayed near a dangerous precipice. And as they walked home in the evening, he explained to them what was happening and told them of his plans for the next day. This encounter with eastern shepherds provided me with a new perspective on the familiar image used by Jesus.

In order to deepen my understanding of Jesus's claim, I turned to the Old Testament and to the descriptions it contains of faithful shepherds.

[The Sovereign Lord] tends his flock like a shepherd; he gathers the lambs in his arms and carries them close to his heart; he gently leads those that have young (Isa. 40:11).

The Sovereign Lord says: I myself will search for my sheep and look after them. As a shepherd looks after his scattered flock... I will search for the lost and bring back the strays. I will bind up the injured and strengthen the weak... (Ezekiel 34:11; 16).

The Lord is my shepherd, I shall not be in want.
He makes me lie down in green pastures,
   he leads me beside quiet waters,
   he restores my soul.
He guides me in paths of righteousness
   for his name's sake.
Even though I walk
   through the valley of the shadow of death,
I fear no evil,
   for you are with me;
your rod and your staff,
   they comfort me (Ps. 23:1–4).

I meditated on these passages for several days. The

picture of the Good Shepherd which rose up before me was of a man who expresses his faithfulness through his availability: 'he leads me, restores me, is with me.' The good shepherd is one who involves himself in the life of his flock: he gathers the lambs together, carries them, leads the ewes with gentleness. The Good Shepherd is a dedicated person: he searches for the lost, heals the sick, bandages the wounded. Communication between sheep and shepherd seemed a two-way affair: the helpless sheep looked to the shepherd for guidance, wisdom and direction. These resources were given constantly. The relationship which grew between a sheep and his shepherd was one of intimacy.

Not only does Jesus *imply* that, as the Good Shepherd, he will communicate with his flock. Here he *promises* that the Holy Spirit will be a talking, teaching, acting agent of God whose mission will be to show us the truth by transmitting God's messages and to further lead us into the truth by revealing to us 'what is yet to come'.

Peter takes up this theme on the day of Pentecost. When he quotes from the prophet Joel he hints that the Holy Spirit has at his disposal a whole variety of ways to ensure that God's will and Word are made known to man:

> In the last days, God says,
> I will pour out my Spirit on all people.
> Your sons and daughters will prophesy,
> your young men will see visions,
> your old men will dream dreams, (Acts 2:17 quoting Joel 2:28).

Paul repeats the refrain in his letter to the Corinthians. The gifts of the Spirit are, in the main, gifts of communication: prophecy, tongues, discernment and knowledge (1 Cor. 12). It is as though Paul is reminding us that the God who yearns to communicate will find a variety of ways to convey God's message and apply God's revealed word to his people. Can this really happen *only* through the text of scripture?

The writer to the Hebrews, quoting from Psalm 95, assumes that God will continue to speak to his people. Three times he quotes the Holy Spirit as saying: Today, *if you hear his voice*, do not harden your hearts...' (Heb. 3:7-8, 15 italics mine).

And John the Divine, contemplating the glorified Lord, builds on the foundations already laid in both the Old Testament and the New. Through him Jesus invites believers and unbelievers alike to hear his voice: 'Here I am! I stand at the door and knock. *If anyone hears my voice* and opens the door, I will come in...' (Rev. 3:20, italics mine).

I turned to the Old Testament. There I noticed God talking to Adam, to Abraham and to Moses 'as a man speaks with his friend' (Exod. 33:11). Similarly, David and Solomon, Elijah and Nathan, to name but a few dignitaries, heard the voice of God.

And my survey of the books of the Bible highlighted another truth. Over and over again, when God communicated with those he loved, it was he who took the initiative, by preceding the person and providing him with an awareness of his presence or speaking in clear unmistakable ways. So the psalmist cried out in wonder, 'Thou, God, seest me.' Jacob acknowledged, 'Surely, the Lord is in this place and I was not aware of it' (Gen. 28:16). Mary Magdalene heard that one, welcome, economical word at the tomb, 'Mary!' And the disciples on the road to Emmaus enjoyed the companionship of the stranger whose company and conversation caused their hearts to burn within them.

Several of Jesus's parables encourage us to expect God to take the initiative in this relationship of love. The father waits and watches for the return of the prodigal and gathers up his skirts so that he is free to run to greet the returning wanderer. The woman searches until she finds the coin she has lost. The good shepherd searches ceaselessly for the sheep who has wandered away.

The more I delved into the pages of the Bible, the more convinced I became that the thread which runs right through the Old Testament and the New is of a God who spoke to his people incisively and intimately in times past, a God who is the same yesterday, today and forever, a God whose constancy and consistency do not permit him to 'change like shifting shadows' (Jas. 1:17), a God who is therefore committed to communicate in creative ways throughout history: through the written word, through his Son (Heb. 1:2), through dreams, through visions, through angels, through the prompting of the indwelling Spirit, through nature, indeed, through any method he chooses. As David Watson puts it: 'God did not finish speaking to us when the scriptures were completed ... God is the living God, the God of today; and every day he wants us to enjoy a living relationship with him, involving a two-way conversation.'[1]

Convinced and thrilled by these early investigations into the Bible's view of listening to God, I read on. The outcome was a whole chapter of surprises.

Chapter 8

Commanded to Listen

The God who spoke in times past still speaks and will continue to speak throughout history. God's word is powerful, full of majesty (Ps. 29:4), accurate and active (Heb. 4:12). These solemn truths overshadowed me as I continued to survey the Bible's teaching on listening to God. Michael Mitton expresses it in this way:

> The life of man is impoverished if he does not communicate with his Creator... Man is created as a responding creature – he must respond to his Maker. By doing this, to use Martin Buber's language, he becomes 'I' as he communicates with 'Thou'. If God does not communicate to us, he is only an 'It'; if he speaks to us, and we speak with him, he becomes 'Thou'.[1]

That God is a 'Thou', a person as opposed to an object, I had no doubt. That God yearns to communicate, similarly, I had no doubt. But what I learned next about the God of the Bible took me by surprise.

I had turned from meditating on the shepherding of Jesus to contemplate the Transfiguration. Embedded in Matthew's account of this unique revelation of Jesus's glory, lay a command which I had never bumped into before: 'There he was transfigured before them. His face shone like the sun, and his clothes became as white as the light... and a voice from the cloud said, "This is my Son, whom I love; with him I am well pleased. *Listen to him!*"' (Matt. 17:2, 5, italics mine).

I looked at this verse long and hard and found it difficult to believe that it does not say, 'This is my dear Son, talk to him.' Nor does it read, 'This is my dear Son, ask him for things.' Neither does it encourage, 'This is my dear Son, tell him your diagnosis when someone is sick.' No. It reads, 'This is my Son... *Listen to him.*'

Why had I never noticed this verse before? Why had I never heard anyone preach a sermon on it? Why was the emphasis always on asking God for things when we pray rather than on listening to him? Did this verse mean simply that God's people are to obey his words which have been recorded in the Bible or does it imply something more than that?

With this clear command to listen to God staring me in the face, these questions puzzled and bothered me. When I unearthed a whole string of commands to listen to God, I became even more perplexed and asked myself why some people claim that it is presumptuous to expect God to speak when God's call to listen runs through the Old Testament and the New in the same way as a theme tune runs through a film.

I found God's call to listen highlighted most movingly in the history of the youth Samuel:

The Lord called Samuel a third time, and Samuel got up and went to Eli and said, 'Here I am; you called me.' Then Eli realised that the Lord was calling the boy. So Eli told Samuel, 'Go and lie down, and if he calls you, say, "Speak, Lord, for your servant is listening."' So Samuel went and lay down in his place. The Lord came and stood there, calling as at the other times, 'Samuel! Samuel!' Then Samuel said, 'Speak, for your servant is listening' (1 Sam. 3:8–10).

The same command to listen punctuates the book of Isaiah: 'Consult me' (30:2); 'Listen' (44:1); 'Hear this...' (51:21); 'Listen to me' (55:2); 'Give ear and come to me; hear me...' (55:3).

Jeremiah takes up the theme: 'Hear the word of the Lord, all... who come through these gates to worship the Lord' (7:2).

And Ezekiel commands nature itself to listen to God: 'Prophesy to these bones and say to them, "Dry bones, hear the word of the Lord!"' (37:4).

The same command to listen throbs through the early chapters of the book of Revelation like a persistent drumbeat:

If you have ears, then, *listen* to what the Spirit says (2:7)

If you have ears, then, *listen* to what the Spirit says (2:11)

If you have ears, then, *listen* to what the Spirit says (2:17)

If you have ears, then, *listen* to what the Spirit says (2:29)

If you have ears, then, *listen* to what the Spirit says (3:6)

I found that, according to Micah, political leaders do not escape the divine interdict: 'Listen... you rulers of the house of Israel! Should you not know justice, you who hate good and love evil' (Mic. 3:1).

Amos reminds rebels to listen: 'Hear this word, you cows of Bashan on Mount Samaria, you women who oppress the poor and crush the needy and say to your husbands, "Bring us some drinks!"' (Amos 4:1).

Old men are exhorted to listen to God. 'Hear this, you elders' (Joel 1:2). Idle women must listen: 'you women who are so complacent, rise up and listen... (Isa. 32:9). Whole families are required to listen: 'Hear the word of the Lord... all you clans of the house of Israel. This is what the Lord says...' (Jer. 2:4). These people were not listening to the written Word only. They were expected to hear and obey God on a day-to-day basis.

The more I burrowed into the Bible, the clearer it became that men and women of God heeded this command; they expected God to speak to them because he had promised to do so and because he had commanded them to listen.

The impression I gained from my study is that men and women in the Bible were not unlike my milkman in one respect. My milkman does his entire round tuned in to a voice other than his own or the cheery comments of his customers. In the pocket of his white, nylon overalls he carries a personal portable radio. Into his ears he tucks its tiny headphones and his face, indeed, sometimes his whole body, responds to a sound which is not audible to anyone but him. Men and women in the Bible seemed similarly plugged into and responsive to God. When they listened and responded obediently to the will of God, their life ran smoothly. When they refused to listen, God's heart broke. God's reaction to man's failure to listen sent a stab of pain right through me and further convinced me of his longing to communicate.

God's disappointment

Jeremiah puts the situation powerfully: 'I spoke to you again and again, but you did not listen; I called you, but you did not answer. Therefore... I will thrust you from my presence, just as I did all your brothers, the people of Ephraim' (Jer. 7:13, 15).

Zechariah, too, exposes the anger which burns in the heart of God when his people refuse to listen.

'My people stubbornly refused to listen. They closed their minds and made their hearts as hard as rock. Because they would not listen to my teaching... I became very angry. Because they did not listen when I spoke, I did not answer when they prayed.' (Zech. 7:10).

And I found God spelling out his displeasure through the lips of Isaiah also:

The people do as they please. It's all the same to them whether they kill a bull as a sacrifice or sacrifice a human being ... They take pleasure in disgusting ways of worship. So I will bring in disaster upon them – the very things they are afraid of – because no one answered when I called or listened when I spoke – They chose to disobey me and do evil. (Isaiah 66:3-4).

Against this back-cloth, I placed the success stories: occasions when the voice of God was obeyed. Two such incidents in Acts thrilled me:

The Spirit told Philip, 'Go to that chariot and stay near it.' Then Philip ran ... (Acts 8:29-30).

The Lord told him [Ananias], 'Go to the house of Judas on Straight Street and ask for a man from Tarsus named Saul, for he is praying. In a vision he has seen a man named Ananias come and place his hands on him to restore his sight.'
... Then Ananias went to the house and entered it. Placing his hands on Saul, he said, 'Brother Saul, the Lord ... has sent me so that you may see again and be filled with the Holy Spirit.' Immediately, something like scales fell from Saul's eyes, and he could see again (Acts 9: 11-12, 17-18).

The result of Philip's obedient listening is well known: the Ethiopian turned to Christ. Similarly, the punch-line of the Saul and Ananias story is familiar: Saul's sight was restored and the direction of his life changed.

I found similar miracles recorded in the gospels. A well-known story fired my imagination:

When evening came, [Jesus] said to his disciples, 'Let us go over to the other side.' Leaving the crowd behind, they took him along, just as he was, in the boat ... A furious squall came up, and the waves broke over the boat, so that it was nearly swamped. Jesus was in the stern, sleeping on a cushion. The disciples woke him and said to him, 'Teacher, don't you care if we drown?'

He got up, rebuked the wind and said to the waves, 'Quiet! Be still!' Then the wind died down and it was completely calm (Mark 4:35–39).

And the terrified disciples asked each other, 'Who is this? Even the wind and the waves obey him!'

Again my mind wandered back to Israel, to an occasion when my husband and I were caught in an unexpected storm on the Sea of Galilee.

We had been lazing on a tiny beach on the shores of the lake. After we had sunbathed, collected miniature shells, imagined Jesus standing in a fishing boat teaching the crowds in the open-air auditorium, and wandered through some wheat fields, we decided to head back for Tiberias.

As we travelled, the weather changed. A grey cloud crept over the sun and spread right across the sky. A wind began to howl from the surrounding hills. And the white pleasure-boat rocked and rolled as the storm whipped the waves into a fury. Unlike the other passengers, David and I braved the wind and the rain and the spray which soaked us as great waves crashed against the sides of the boat. Perhaps we had hoped to live through a sudden squall like this? It helped us identify with the disciples' panic. It also stirred in our hearts a sense of wonder as we realised that Jesus had only to speak to giant waves like this. They heard. They subsided.

No voice silenced the storm that day, yet I recalled that Jesus is still the sustainer of the universe. He still holds the whole world in his hand. The cosmos is still dependent for its existence 'on every word that comes from the mouth of God' (Matt. 4:4).

The facts before me seemed inescapable. The Bible does address itself to the subject of listening to God. Indeed, the God of the Bible is portrayed as a God who aches to communicate: he promises to speak, he commands the entire world to listen. When we refuse, we hurt and anger him, but when we obey, he showers us and others with undeserved and unexpected gifts. But what of this counter-claim that the only method God now uses to speak is through his revealed Word, the Bible?

I thought long and hard about this while I tramped the hills of Derbyshire one day. 'Is it possible to hold in tension two apparently opposite and opposing view-points?' I wondered. As I walked and wondered, certain facts clarified in my mind:

* God has spoken.

* Christianity is a revealed religion.

* In his written Word, the Bible, and the incarnate Word, Jesus, God has given full expression of the fundamentals and foundations of our faith.

* As Christians, therefore, we shall not expect to receive any further revelation of *doctrine*.

* The Bible contains the complete Word of God and everything must be tested by this yard-stick.

But does this full and complete revelation condemn a Creator-God to silence? I looked at the hills which I love. I gazed at the sky which was changing in colour from pearl to purple, then to pink. And the force of the 'Surely not!' which burst into my brain took me by surprise.

To suggest that this full and complete revelation which we have in scripture condemns a Creator-God to silence would be like denying the same God the creativity of the seasons, or saying that he must paint the sky the same colour every night at sunset.

I looked again at the familiar hills and the nearby woods, and I recollected that every time I go to Derbyshire, a place to which I frequently retreat to write, 'my' hills and woods are always the same, yet fascinatingly different. These hills which were created 'in the beginning' by God are still subjects of his artistic flair. In winter, they are sometimes snow-hushed, in autumn they are resplendent in their russets and reds, in spring the virgin greens which clothe the countryside cause us to catch our breath in wonder every year.

God created; and God still creates. Similarly, God has spoken; and God still speaks. This was the conclusion I reached. When we listen to God, we do not expect God to say anything new *doctrinally*. Of course not, the doctrine of our faith has been spelt out by God once and for all. What we do expect is that, when we listen to God, the indwelling Holy Spirit will speak to the situation in which we find ourselves, but whatever comes from him will be in alignment with the Bible's teaching.

I checked this conclusion with my husband on one occasion. I have always respected his integrity and unwavering faithfulness to the Word of God. I knew that he, too, was learning to value some of the insights on prayer which I had gleaned and which he could tell were of increasing value to my spiritual life. As we talked, he seemed to put his finger on the nub of the matter with a memorable observation: 'Listening to God is not about *newness* but about *nowness*. It is receiving the applied Word in whatever form God chooses to make it known.'

For me, that summed up the situation well. The hurt and anxiety with which I had begun my study on listening to God vanished. I was convinced that claims like the one Richard Foster makes are correct: 'Jesus Christ is alive and here to teach his people himself. His voice is not hard to hear, his vocabulary is not hard to understand. But we must learn how to hear his voice and obey it.'[2]

In the light of this conviction, I set myself the joyful task of learning God's vocabulary. The prayer Eli taught Samuel found an echo in my own heart: 'Speak, Lord, for your servant is listening' (1 Sam. 3:9).

Chapter 9

How God speaks: Visions and Dreams

'Man needs every word that God speaks.' Commenting on this claim, David Watson observes: 'The word "speaks" (ekporeuomeno) means "is continually coming out of" the mouth of God. Since God is the living God, he is constantly trying to speak to us and we in turn need to listen to him . . . If we are to keep spiritually alive and alert, we need every word that God is continually speaking.'[1]

Anxious as I was to 'keep spiritually alive and alert', indeed, to grow in Christian maturity, statements like this tickled my taste-buds. And now that I had established for myself that the Bible gives positive encouragement to the Christian not only to listen to God's written Word, the Bible, but also to attune to the living Word, the Spirit of Jesus, I was eager to forge ahead in the discipline of listening.

The kind of pondering on God which the gift of contemplation had opened up for me featured for several key people in the Bible. After Jesus's circumcision, Mary and Joseph 'marvelled' (Luke 2:33). After Jesus's first visit to Jerusalem as a boy, we read that 'his mother treasured all these things in her heart' (Luke 2:51). To marvel and to treasure the mysteries of the faith is contemplation. The apostle John, similarly, contemplated the mysteries of the faith in the gloom of the empty tomb on the morning of the Resurrection: 'He saw and believed' (John 20:8) implies that he contemplated the strips of linen used to embalm Jesus's body and slowly the realisation dawned that what Jesus had predicted had, in fact, happened. Similarly, we find Simeon contemplating the Christ child: 'Simeon took him in his arms and praised God, saying: . . . "My eyes have seen your salvation"' (Luke 2:28; 30). This is no cursory glance Simeon is referring to. It is the long, lingering, adoring gaze of the contemplative at prayer. The Old Testament, too, teems with images which highlight the art of contemplation: 'Lord, you have been our dwelling place' (Ps. 90:1); 'He who dwells in the shelter of the Most High will rest in the shadow of the Almighty' (Ps. 91:1); 'He will cover you with his feathers, and under his wings you will find refuge' (Ps. 91:4). Daniel, Isaiah, Ezekiel and Moses knew what it meant to lose themselves in the awesomeness of adoring, listening prayer.

But God has a variety of methods of communication at his fingertips. A quick glance at the Old Testament and the New convinced me that God frequently conveyed his purpose and plan to man pictorially as well as verbally. The vision seemed to be a favourite means of communication.

By profession, I am a teacher of the deaf. I reflected that when I used to teach deaf children, it would never occur to me to try to teach them anything without some form of visual aid. Communication experts assure us that we remember what we see far more permanently than we store the words we hear. In the light of this, I was fascinated to find God transmitting very ordinary messages to his people by means of a method which we pride ourselves is 'modern'.

It was through a vision that God promised the veteran couple, Abraham and Sara, that they would give birth to a much longed-for baby:

After this, the word of the Lord came to Abram in a

vision: 'Do not be afraid, Abram. I am your shield, your very great reward' . . .

And Abram said, 'You have given me no children; so a servant in my household will be my heir.'

Then the word of the Lord came to him: 'This man will not be your heir, but a son coming from your own body will be your heir.'

He took him outside and said, 'Look up at the heavens and count the stars – if indeed you can count them.' Then he said to him, 'So shall your offspring be' (Genesis 15:1, 3–5).

Isaiah, similarly, received his life-changing vocation through a memorable vision:

In the year that King Uzziah died, I saw the Lord seated on a throne, high and exalted, and the train of his robe filled the temple. Above him were the seraphs, each with six wings: with two wings they covered their faces, with two they covered their feet, and with two they were flying. And they were calling to one another: 'Holy, holy, holy is the Lord Almighty; the whole earth is full of his glory.'

At the sound of the voices the doorposts and thresholds shook and the temple was filled with smoke.

'Woe to me!' I cried. 'I am ruined! For I am a man of unclean lips . . .'

Then one of the seraphs flew to me with a live coal in his hand, . . . With it he touched my mouth and said, 'See, this has touched your lips; your guilt is taken away and your sin atoned for.'

Then I heard the voice of the Lord saying, 'Whom shall I send? And who will go for us?'

And I said, 'Here am I. Send me!' (Isa. 6:1–8).

In the New Testament, God continues to use this colourful and profound method of communication. He used it to impress on Peter the fact that God is not simply a God for the Jews but rather a God whose salvation embraces gentiles also. The picture God gave Peter to prepare him for this revelation is curious:

> Peter went up on the roof to pray. He became hungry and wanted something to eat, and while the meal was being prepared, he fell into a trance. He saw heaven opened and something like a large sheet being let down to earth by its four corners. It contained all kinds of four-footed animals, as well as reptiles of the earth and birds of the air. Then a voice told him, 'Get up, Peter. Kill and eat.'
>
> 'Surely not, Lord!' Peter replied. 'I have never eaten anything impure or unclean.'
>
> The voice spoke to him a second time, 'Do not call anything impure that God has made clean' (Acts 10:9–14).

Luke records that while Peter was still thinking through the implications of this startling mental picture, three men arrived on his door step asking Peter's help for the gentile, Cornelius. The Holy Spirit gave Peter clear instructions: 'Do not hesitate to go with them, for I have sent them' (Acts 10:20). Little by little, the message concealed in God's picture emerges. When Cornelius makes his request for instruction in the Christian faith, Peter understands why the vision occurred when it did and in the way it did. He makes this comment to Cornelius: 'You are well aware that it is against our law for a Jew to associate with a gentile or visit him. But God has shown me that I should not call any man impure or unclean' (Acts 10:28).

Through this pictorial message, God had liberated Peter from the prejudices and perspectives of his upbringing. The economy and dynamic of these pictures with the immediacy and urgency of their message made a deep impression on me. It seemed a powerful and unforgettable way for God to make his will and way known to his people.

Other visions seemed to fall into a different category. These were glimpses of God's glory and future kingdom given to ordinary men by God while they were 'in the Spirit', gazing at God alone. Daniel records the revelation God gave him: 'I looked up and there before me was a man dressed in linen, with a belt of the finest gold round his waist. His body was like chrysolite, his face like lightning, his eyes like flaming torches, his arms and legs like the gleam of burnished bronze, and his voice like the sound of a multitude' (Dan. 10:5-6).

And he tells us what he heard from the man's lips: '"Now I have come to explain to you what will happen to your people in the future, for the vision concerns a time yet to come"' (Dan. 10:14).

Ezekiel, similarly, met a man in a vision 'whose appearance was like bronze; he was standing in the gateway with a linen cord and a measuring rod in his hand...' (Ezek. 40:3). Ezekiel's vision with its detailed description of the temple he saw, takes up pages of his book.

In contrast, some visions seemed ordinary, almost mundane: 'The word of the Lord came to me: "What do you see, Jeremiah?"

"I see the branch of an almond tree," I replied' (Jer. 1:11).

That kind of vision encouraged me because it seemed more attainable than the extravagance of Isaiah's vision or the revelation of God's glory which John describes in his last book of the Bible, or the double-edged prophecy which Daniel goes on to give in Daniel 10.

While this academic appraisal of visions was in progress, I began to talk to people about visions to discover whether God still speaks in this way today. I was soon to discover that God did not stop using this technicolour language when the last full stop was added to the book of Revelation. He is still comforting and cajoling and challenging people through this medium today.

A friend of mine explained to me how God had met her in the depths of despair through a vision.

She was married to a pastor but had indulged in an affair with a married man. Eventually, the realisation dawned that she had reached a cross-roads. Either she must leave her husband and children and cause untold hurt to numerous people, or she must give up her lover. She chose the latter.

Having repented of the illicit love-affair, she wandered into the woods to think and to pray. As she continued to pour out the bitterness of her soul to God, she described her life to him as nothing more than fragments of her former self. While she stood, silent and still before God, into her mind came a picture of the fragments she had described: they littered the ground like so many pieces of red clay. As she gazed at the broken vessel representing her life, into the picture came Jesus. She saw the tenderness of his face and observed the sensitivity of his fingers as he stooped down and started to turn over those forlorn fragments. 'Suddenly, he started to piece them together,' she told me. 'He assured me that, though the vessel was a mess, every tiny piece of the pot was precious. I watched the skill with which he put the pieces together again. He re-created that vessel. He showed me that it would be even more beautiful than it had been before and much more useful. Then, he glazed it and held it up for me to see. I couldn't see a single sign of the joins where the cracked parts had been pressed back together.'

For that woman, this vision came to her as a promise from God which guaranteed her future with him. It also communicated the much-needed message of healing and forgiveness which motivated her to walk away from the sin of the past and to work at her marriage again.

God had already spoken to this woman through his

written Word. When she first confessed her sin to him and repented of it, she turned to 1 John 1:9: 'If we confess our sins, he is faithful and just and will forgive us our sins and purify us from all unrighteousness.' She believed this revealed Word. In her head she knew that God had forgiven her. But sexual sin affects not our heads only, but our entire being: body, mind, personality, emotions, imagination, spirit. God knows this. The series of images he planted into this woman's sin-saddened mind touched her in a way words never could. The vividness of the vision engraved God's revealed truth on to her heart and set her free to become the gifted person for him he had always intended that she should be.

It was not long before God began to give me mental pictures like the one which had transformed my friend's life. Sometimes these would come while I was still before God and in prayer. Often these would build up my faith or deepen my awareness of God's presence. On one occasion, while I was praying, a picture of a beautiful oasis rose before my eyes. The water in the pond was still and pure; the trees which surrounded it were stately and offered shade from the scorching sun. Beside the pond stood an animal: a deer which seemed to be looking for something. When a fawn appeared, the deer showed his delight. They nudged each other affectionately. The fawn snuggled into the deer's warm body. They drank together from the pool before resting in the warm grass. When I asked God what this delightful picture meant, he seemed to assure me that this was a representation of my listening prayer. The time I set aside to develop my relationship with him becomes an oasis. In this still place he waits, more eager for an encounter with me than I am to encounter him. He seemed to show me that on the occasions when I come to this place of refreshment, I must be unashamed to delight in him; that he, similarly, will show me that he delights in me; that I am the focus of his love, the object of his affection and care. During these times he would nourish me. Like the bride in the Song of Songs I would sit under his shade and taste the fruit of his love.

On other occasions, a picture would unfold in my mind while I was counselling. On those occasions, the counselling interview would often be far more incisive and effective than when I was relying on counselling skills only. I began to realise that these visions were promptings from the Holy Spirit which frequently brought me to the heart of the person's need.

I remember praying for a girl on one occasion who was sobbing uncontrollably yet unable to voice the anguish the tears were trying to express. While I prayed silently for her and she continued to weep, I saw in my mind's eye the picture of a little girl in a playground at school. Her play-mates were teasing her mercilessly.

When the girl stopped crying, I described the school scene to her and asked her if it made any sense. 'Why, yes!' she exclaimed. 'That's me. I'd forgotten all about it but I used to be teased at school such a lot.'

This picture proved to be the key which unlocked the door into the emotional hurt which was paralysing this young Christian. I marvelled. God had shown me in seconds what counselling might have taken weeks to disclose.

Dreams
The borderline between visions and dreams is thumb-nail thin. When a person sees a vision, he sees a series of images while he is wide awake and attentive to the Holy Spirit. When a person dreams, on the other hand, he, too, sees a series of images but does so while he is fast asleep.

As I delved into the Bible to discover how frequently God resorted to this means of conveying a message, I was taken by surprise. I found that the book of Numbers implies that visions and dreams are perfectly valid means of prophetic revelation: 'When a prophet of the Lord is among you, I reveal myself to him in visions, I speak to him in dreams' (Num. 12:6). I found that Jeremiah endorses the fact that a prophet might receive a prophetic dream: 'Let the prophet who has a dream tell his dream' (Jer. 23:28). Indeed, Jeremiah himself describes such a dream in which God describes the peace and harmony and obedience which he will bestow on his chosen people (Jer. 31: 26). And Joel foresees the day when God's Spirit will be poured out on all mankind and when the links between prophecy, dreams and visions will be crystal clear:

I will pour out my Spirit on all people.
Your sons and daughters will prophesy,
   your old men will dream dreams,
   your young men will see visions. (Joel 2:28 quoted in
   Acts 2:17).

Dreams feature frequently in the New Testament. Matthew, for example, records several dreams in connection with the birth of Jesus. God spoke to Joseph through a dream on two occasions: in the first, to instruct him to go through with his intended marriage to Mary and, in the second, to advise him that Herod's death had paved the way for the family to return to Nazareth. Similarly, it is through a dream that the magi received God's warning not to return home by the proposed route, by way of Herod's palace, but to travel a different way from the way they had come. And later in the gospel Matthew refers to the dream which threw Pilate's wife into turmoil: '"Don't have anything to do with that innocent man [Jesus], for I have suffered a great deal today in a dream because of him"' (Matt. 27:19).

With this data in front of me, I began to reflect on a vivid dream I had had on the last day of a sun-splashed holiday in Greece one spring.

With David and Kevin and Christina, our children, I had shoe-horned myself into the cabin of the passenger boat which ploughs between the island of Rhodes and

Athens. We had torn ourselves away from the delights of Lindos with its tiny harbour, its cobbled streets, its colourful bazaars and its famous donkey transport. After the night voyage, we would collect our dormobile and start the long haul home by road.

That night my sleep was disturbed by a dream in which I saw our dormobile being towed away by a lorry. The vehicle was a total wreck. In the dream, I watched the rescue lorry disappear from sight taking most of our possessions with it.

I woke from that dream, lay in the darkness and, with uncharacteristic calm, prayed: 'Lord, if that should happen to us, please give me the courage to cope.' The prayer offered, with a peace which does not match my personality, I fell asleep.

On the following day, in high spirits, I drove from Athens to Skopje in Yugoslavia where I handed the driving over to my husband. The dream forgotten, I settled on to the back seat of the dormobile to read the map and relax. I don't know what made me glance up at my husband. What I do remember is the grim, grey look on his face as I watched him juggle with a steering wheel which clearly was out of control. With incredulity, I watched him drive through mid-air and head for a silver-birch tree. I heard my nine-year-old daughter scream, 'No! No!' And I felt the dormobile bounce off the trunk of the tree before somersaulting down the steep embankment.

Some minutes later, I lay on the grassy bank, conscious of a dull pain between my shoulder blades, aware of blood pouring from a head wound and staring at the twisted machinery before me which six months earlier had been our brand new, blue Volkswagen dormobile. But I was not surprised. Nor shaken. It was as though I had lived this moment the night before in my dream. This was simply an action replay of a familiar event. Through the trauma of the chaotic days which followed, my heart stayed at peace.

Two days later, while I lay in a primitive hospital north

of Skopje wearing a crown of bandages on my injured head, a lorry towed the dormobile containing most of our possessions to the scrap heap – just as my dream had foretold.

While I was regaining strength in this hospital, news filtered through that my father had died tragically and suddenly of a heart attack. By the time we reached home, the funeral was over. I was never able to say my final farewell to him.

My husband referred to the accident and the bereavement and the dream in a sermon on one occasion soon after we arrived back in England. A surgeon happened to be in the congregation that morning. After the service, he told my husband something which we had not appreciated at the time: that if someone was to suffer the kind of head injuries I sustained and be so quickly subjected to the added pain of bereavement, this dream was the kindest possible preparation they could have. The trust the dream engendered ensured that, at the time of the tragedies, I was relaxed, conscious that I was held by a love which would not let me go.

Thinking back to that time, I remembered that when my husband had passed on this piece of medical information my heart had missed a beat. I had wanted, there and then, to believe that this dream had originated with God, that through it he had been assuring me of his protective love and constant care. But I had never allowed this to take root. I had been taught that God speaks to us only through the Bible, not through dreams. But now that that shibboleth was becoming a notion of my past, and in the light of the facts before me – that God's use of dreams was a well-tried and often-occurring method of communication – I was forced to re-evaluate the situation. Like Mary, I marvelled at God's faithfulness and treasured this memory with its hidden message of love, constancy and compassion.

John Sherrill, in his introduction to Herman Riffel's

book on dreams, makes the claim that dreams are a secret code and advises that we learn to unravel this code.[2] Herman Riffel believes that dreams can 'be a valuable computer in a man's unconscious realm'.[3] I do not have sufficient insight into dreams and their interpretations to assess whether these claims are accurate or not. What I do know is that, in the past, God used dreams to transmit messages to his people. What I also now know is that, on one occasion at least, he has spoken to me in this way.

Chapter 10

How God Speaks: Voices and Angels

When a man catches a glimpse of God's glory through a vision it is but a fragment of that full revelation of God which we shall enjoy when we meet him face to face. And when a man encounters God in a dream this is but a pale reflection of the splendour we shall one day savour. Nevertheless, such revelations are to be recognised for what they often are: manifestations of God's presence, his tap at the window of our souls.

But God does not always resort to picture parables when he wants to make his purposes known. My Bible survey suggested to me that a favourite means of message transmission was nothing less than the clear, unmistakable, uncompromising voice of God communicating clearly with his people.

Indeed God reminds Aaron and Miriam that it is his intention to speak to certain people in this way:

When a prophet of the Lord is among you,
I reveal myself to him in visions,
I speak to him in dreams.
But this is not true of my servant Moses . . .
With him I speak face to face,
    clearly and not in riddles;
    he sees the form of the Lord (Num. 12:6–8).

Moreover, the Bible is full of references to situations in which other individuals heard God speak, not through pictures, which always require an interpretation, but through an uncontrived conversation with God. Noah heard God's voice: 'God said to Noah, "I am going to put an end to all people . . . So make yourself an ark of cypress"' (Gen. 6:13, 14). Similarly Abraham heard God's voice: 'God tested Abraham . . . God said, "Take your son, your only son, Isaac . . . Sacrifice him."' (Gen. 22:1, 2). And Adam heard God's call: 'The Lord God called to the man, "Where are you"' (Gen. 3:9). God spoke to the prophets in this crystal clear manner: 'The word of the Lord that came to Hosea . . . "Go, take to yourself an adulterous wife and children of unfaithfulness"' (Hos. 1:1, 2). 'The word of the Lord came to me, saying, "Before I formed you in the womb I knew you, before you were born I set you apart' (Jer. 1:4). 'The word of the Lord came to him [Elijah]: "Go at once to Zarephath of Sidon and stay there"' (1 Kgs. 17:8–9).

The same awareness of God's voice is recorded in the New Testament. As might be expected, Jesus himself heard it, as Peter testifies: 'For he received honour and glory from God the Father when the voice came to him from the Majestic Glory, saying, "This is my Son, whom I love; with him I am well pleased." We ourselves heard this voice that came from heaven when we were with him on the sacred mountain' (2 Pet. 1:17–18).

Saul heard it as he travelled along the road to Damascus:

As he neared Damascus on his journey, suddenly a light from heaven flashed around him. He fell to the ground and heard a voice say to him, 'Saul, Saul, why do you persecute me?'

'Who are you, Lord?' Saul asked.

'I am Jesus, whom you are persecuting,' he replied (Acts 9:3–5).

John heard it after he had been exiled to the Island of Patmos: 'On the Lord's Day I was in the Spirit, and I heard behind me a loud voice like a trumpet, which said: "Write on a scroll what you see and send it to the seven churches..."' (Rev. 1:10–11).

Isaiah seems to hold out a promise that future generations will also hear that voice. 'Whether you turn to the right or to the left, your ears will hear a voice behind you, saying, "This is the way; walk in it"' (Isa. 30:21). And Jesus reinforced that message by implying that his gentle inspirations and awakenings would continue: '[My sheep] will listen to my voice' (John 10:16); by guaranteeing, too, that the voice of his Spirit would never be silenced. 'But when he, the Spirit of truth, comes, he will guide you into all truth. He will not speak on his own; he will speak only what he hears, and he will tell you what is yet to come' (John 16:13).

Since this voice peals so persistently through the pages of the Bible and since Jesus at least hints that it would never be lost, it seemed relevant to investigate whether that same voice is still being heard today. I soon discovered several people who claimed that they had heard God speaking to them. Indeed, just as I was about to write this chapter, a woman came to tell me of an experience of that voice which had changed the direction of her life.

The woman, an unbeliever, lay in her hospital bed knowing that she was suffering from cancer. In intense pain, she longed for the injection which would prepare her for the operation she was to undergo that afternoon. Since there was no sign of the nurse, she lay back on her pillow, closed her eyes and tried to relax. All of a sudden, standing by her bedside, she 'saw' a priest and another person whom she took to be Jesus. Jesus stretched out his hand and held hers. A calmness spread through her body. Jesus invited her to trust him for the future. She promised him that if she recovered from the anaesthetic, she would live life his way. She did survive. And she kept her promise. She had come to excite me with the delicacies of her new-found faith in God. Over the months I have watched her change even more. She has certainly turned her back on the past and turned to face the living God.

Or I think of a woman I met in Singapore. She told me of a holiday she and her husband planned on the tropical island of Penang. Their flight was booked. Their cases were packed. But on the day of the trip, a voice seemed to urge this woman not to travel by the planned flight. She telephoned her husband and persuaded him to cancel the trip. He did. That day, the air-bus travelling from Singapore to Penang crashed killing all the passengers.

I sense I sometimes hear that voice myself. One Sunday night, I had prayed for a young man whose spirits had sunk very low. Early on Monday morning, I woke with this young man's need weighing heavy on my heart. As I prayed for him, I decided to telephone before he left for work to assure him of my continued prayer. 'I'll ring at eight,' I decided, and started to work on a book I was writing. At 7.45a.m. a voice broke in on my concentration: 'Ring now!' I looked at my watch and decided there was no hurry. But the voice repeated: 'Ring now.' I rang. The young man thanked me for ringing when I told him the purpose of the call. 'Perfect timing too!' he teased. 'Why? When do you leave for work?' I asked. 'Oh! In two minutes' time,' he said. When I heard this, I offered silent praise to the God who, I believe, prompted me to act in time.

Or I recall one harvest time when again God's voice burst in on my awareness and changed my carefully made plans for the day. On the day after the harvest services in our church, members of staff distribute gifts of flowers and fruit to the elderly. When I was parcelling up these gifts, the voice told me first to visit a lady who had recently been widowed and then to call on one of the pensioners attached to the church.

When the widow opened her door, she clung to me. She

was sorting through her husband's possessions and had longed for company and someone to pray with her. A similar scene greeted me on the second visit. That morning the pensioner had received a letter telling her that her sister, to whom she was very close, had suffered a nervous breakdown. When I arrived she was still reading and re-reading this letter, still trying to drink in the tragic news. She, too, had longed for a listening ear and some prayer support. I returned home that day marvelling at God's faithfulness, deeply thankful that he had shunted me into the right place at the right time to be the funnel through which his consolation could be poured.

While I was concentrating on the God who takes the initiative in communicating to his people, through dreams and visions and voices and a whole variety of other ways, God seemed to bring across my path illustration after illustration which suggested to me that he has never, in fact, been silent. There was the mystic, Julian of Norwich, whose revelations of divine love are an unashamed attempt to pass on to others what she believed God had said and shown to her. There was St Francis of Assisi whose personal encounter with the living Lord turned his life inside out. There was St Augustine, whom his mother Monica despaired of, but whose experience of God proved so overwhelming that he cried out in response: 'Too late have I loved thee . . .' And there was St Symeon, a theologian of the eleventh century, who tells how Christ revealed himself in a vision of light:

> You shone upon me with brilliant radiance and, so it seemed, you appeared to me in your wholeness as with my whole self I gazed openly upon you. And when I said, 'Master, who are you?' then you were pleased to speak for the first time with me, the prodigal. With what gentleness did you talk to me, as I stood astonished and trembling, as I reflected a little within myself and said: 'What does this glory and this dazzling brightness

mean? How is it that I am chosen to receive such great blessings?' 'I am God,' you replied, 'who became man for your sake; and because you have sought me with your whole heart, see from this time onwards you shall be my brother, my fellow-heir and my friend.'[1]

All down the ages, it seems God has spoken.

Angels

So far, the truths I was unearthing from the pages of the Bible, from history and from personal testimonies, my own and other people's, thrilled me to the core of my being and caused the level of expectation within me to soar to new heights. But when I bumped into angelology, a systematic statement of biblical truth about angels, my reaction was different. I did not want to believe in angels.

Did my resistance stem from the fact that I had frequently been an angel in nativity plays at school and had therefore relegated these heavenly beings with their shining countenances and translucent wings to the world of make-believe or fantasy? Was it that I had never, to my knowledge, met a single Christian who believed in the existence of angels? Or was it because I feared that an angel was a kind of 'spiritual will-o'-the-wisp', to borrow Billy Graham's phrase, a figment of man's imagination?

I don't know why my resistance to angels was so strong. What I do know is that my survey of the scriptures persuaded me that if I was to be a Bible-believing Christian, it was imperative that I take the belief in angels seriously. The Bible does. Moreoever, the Bible leaves us in no doubt about the nature and purpose of the existence of these heavenly beings.

Angels, according to the author of the letter to the Hebrews, are 'ministering spirits sent to serve those who will inherit salvation' (Heb. 1:14). Myriads of these exotic, glorious, non-material beings shuttle through the pages of the Bible fulfilling their ambassadorial vocation; they offer guidance and give specific instructions to men:

> See, I am sending an angel ahead of you to guard you
> along the way and to bring you to the place I have
> prepared. Pay attention to him and listen to what he
> says. Do not rebel against him ... since my name is in
> him (Exod. 23:20-21).

> An angel of the Lord appeared to Joseph in a dream.
> 'Get up,' he said, 'take the child and his mother and
> escape to Egypt' (Matt. 2:13).

They give advance warning of certain events:

> The angel of the Lord appeared to her and said, 'You are
> sterile and childless, but you are going to conceive and
> have a son' (Judg. 13:3).

> The angel said to her, 'Do not be afraid, Mary, you have
> found favour with God. You will be with child and give
> birth to a son, and you are to give him the name Jesus'
> (Luke 1:30).

They protect and deliver God's people:

> The angel of the Lord encamps around those who fear
> him, and he delivers them (Ps. 34:7).

They are messengers of God's mercy and promise, God's
secret agents:

> While I was still in prayer, Gabriel ... came to me in
> swift flight ... He instructed me and said to me, 'Daniel,
> I have now come to give you insight and understanding'
> (Dan. 9:21-22).

These divine beings, appointed by God to be extensions

of his right hand, usually appear in human form, like the three strangers who descended, without warning, on Abraham and Sara (Gen. 18). It seems that sometimes their voice is heard even though they, themselves, remain invisible (Gen. 21:17).

These spokesmen sent from God stunned me by their glory and silenced my unbelief. I was forced to admit that, in the days when the Bible was penned, angels existed, angels spoke and angels acted.

But does God still send angels? This question puzzled me as I pressed on with my investigation into the methods God chooses to speak today.

I had never seen an angel. Neither did I know anyone who had seen one. But I started to read Billy Graham's thrilling book, *Angels: God's Secret Agents*, and realised that he, at least, is in no doubt that God still communicates through these heavenly beings, who still appear in human form today. To prove it, he records one of God's modern miracles:

The Reverend John G Paton, a missionary in the New Hebrides Islands, tells a thrilling story involving the protective care of angels. Hostile natives surrounded his mission headquarters one night, intent on burning the Patons out and killing them. John Paton and his wife prayed all during that terror-filled night that God would deliver them. When daylight came they were amazed to see the attackers unaccountably leave. They thanked God for delivering them.

A year later, the chief of the tribe was converted to Jesus Christ, and Mr Paton, remembering what had happened, asked the chief what had kept him and his men from burning down the house and killing them. The chief replied in surprise, 'Who were all those men you had with you there?' The missionary answered, 'There were no men there; just my wife and I.' The chief argued that they had seen many men standing guard –

hundreds of big men in shining garments with drawn
swords in their hands. They seemed to circle the mission
station so that the natives were afraid to attack. Only
then did Mr Paton realise that God had sent his angels to
protect them. The chief agreed that there was no other
explanation. Could it be that God had sent a legion of
angels to protect his servants, whose lives were being
endangered?[2]

A shiver of excitement ran down my spine as I read story
after story like this in Billy Graham's book. It would seem
that God still sends his agents to protect and direct us:

When I was visiting the American troops during the
Korean war, I was told of a small group of American
marines in the First Division who had been trapped up
north. With the thermometer at 20° below zero, they
were close to freezing to death. And they had had
nothing to eat for six days. Surrender to the Chinese
seemed their only hope of survival. But one of the men, a
Christian, pointed out certain verses of scripture and
taught his comrades to sing a song of praise to God.
Following this they heard a crashing noise, and turned
to see a wild boar rushing towards them. As they tried to
jump out of his way, he suddenly stopped in his tracks.
One of the soldiers raised his rifle to shoot, but before he
could fire, the boar inexplicably toppled over. They
rushed up to kill him only to find that he was already
dead. That night they feasted on meat, and began to
regain strength.

The next morning, just as the sun was rising, they
heard another noise. Their fear that a Chinese patrol
had discovered them suddenly vanished as they found
themselves face to face with a South Korean who could
speak English. He said, 'I will show you out.' He led
them through the forest and mountains to safety behind

their own lines. When they looked up to thank him, they found he had disappeared.[3]

Testimonies like these, placed against the backdrop of biblical teaching which had already convinced me of the existence of angels, transformed my prayer life. At first this amounted to no more than an inclusion of the mention of them in vocal prayer: 'Lord, send your angels to protect us as we travel.' It wasn't until the first draft of this chapter had been written that I 'saw' an angel in prayer.

I was suffering from a severe and unexpected bout of depression which left me curiously insecure. The situation eventually distressed me so much that I asked two friends to pray with me. The night before we had agreed to meet, I asked God to show me if there was anything from my past which was blurring my perspective of the present. At 4.00a.m. I woke up re-living a vivid memory from my teen years. I was in a beauty spot in Devonshire where I had lived at the time. I could see the sun shining through the beech leaves, hear the brook gurgling its way down the gorge, feel the firmness of the stepping stones on which I had stood to contemplate this beauty. But a chill cloud passed over the entire scene as I became conscious of a man approaching me whose look was sinister, whose intentions clearly were far from pure, who put his arm around my shoulders and tried to kiss me. At this stage of the action replay, I froze and switched the memory off. It had become too painful to watch alone.

That evening, I told my friends about this memory. We recognised that seeds of distrust had been sown on that occasion when this man, a so-called friend, had planned to molest me. They asked God to touch my memory and to remove from it anything which would distort my view of people in the present and leave me with feelings of insecurity.

The sense of evil stayed with me for several days. At times, I seemed to be overwhelmed and over-shadowed by

it: the same sense of evil which had spoiled the beauty of
that lovely day in Devon. One morning, in the stillness of
my prayer corner, again I re-lived the memory. It seemed
important that I should do so. This time, I saw not only
myself standing on the stepping stone and my assailant
coming towards me: this time, I also saw an angel
standing on the same stepping stone as me. His
outstretched wings formed a shelter into which I could
creep. I knew that under his wings I could find safety. The
voice of God seemed to come to me clearly. I recorded them
in my prayer journal:

> Joyce! Think not so much of the powers of evil
> The powers of destruction
> But of my power to protect.
> I watched over you
> I shielded you from harm
> I held you in *my* arms
> The arms of pure love.
> In this relax and rejoice
> For I am your God
> And you are the apple of my eye.
> I am your God
> Your best interests are tucked into the
>   creases of my Father-heart
> I am your Father.

And the words of Psalm 91 rang in my ears like a peal of
joyful bells:

> He will cover you with his feathers,
>   and under his wings you will find refuge;
>   his faithfulness will be your shield and rampart.
> You will not fear the terror of night,
>   nor the arrow that flies by day . . .
> then no harm will befall you . . .

For he will command his angels concerning you
  to guard you in all your ways;
they will lift you up in their hands,
  so that you will not strike your foot against a stone . : .
'Because he loves me,' says the Lord, 'I will
  rescue him' . . .
I will be with him in trouble.

The sense of wonder which filled me was as profound as
the pain had been. Though the memory had bruised me
emotionally, standing in the wake of the brightness of
God's messenger, the angel, and sheltering under the
protection of his wings, brought healing and peace. Some
weeks later, I happened to drive past that particular beauty
spot in Devonshire. As I did so, I noted that the fear and
dread had vanished. I could see the grandeur of God's
creation and praise him for it and remember the past with
peace.

God still uses angels, it seems, to speak even to someone
as cynical about their existence as I had been. And when
God speaks, no matter what method he uses, the encounter
proves powerful. Anthony Bloom puts it well: 'It is
possible to lend an ear to the Living God who speaks to us
and then all other thoughts die out, all other emotions
come to an end because he who is life, he who is the Word,
speaks.'[4]

Chapter 11

How God Speaks: Through Nature and the Imagination

'God speaks to those who keep silence.'[1] God speaks through visions and dreams, through angels, and with a voice as penetrating as the sound of a trumpet. And God also speaks through nature.

When I came to terms with the fact that the created world exists, not simply for our enjoyment, but as a language, my heart did a little, gleeful, hop, skip and a jump. I love nature: the first aconites heralding spring, ripening lilac, scarlet poppies, a mackerel sky. If these could speak to me of God in a deeper way than I had experienced so far, in a way which actually brought me to the Creator, there was a whole unexplored dialect right on my doorstep which I was eager to learn.

Down the ages, I recollected, men and women have heard God speak through the eloquence of nature. God spoke to David in this way so powerfully that the psalmist was inspired to pen Psalm 8:

When I consider your heavens,
    the work of your fingers,
the moon and the stars,
    which you have set in place,
what is man that you are mindful of him? (Ps. 8: 3-4).

Through Isaiah, God challenged his people to contemplate creation:

> Who has measured the waters in the hollow of his hand,
> or with the breadth of his hand marked off the heavens?
> Who has held the dust of the earth in a basket,
> or weighed the mountains on the scales
>   and the hills in a balance? . . .
>
> Surely the nations are like a drop in a bucket;
> they are regarded as dust on the scales;
> he weighs the islands as though they were fine dust . . .
> Before him all the nations are as nothing (Isa. 40:12,
> 15,17).

God, similarly, invited Job to look away from the
darkness within his own soul to the objective orderliness
and beauty of the created world:

> Who shut up the sea behind doors
>   when it burst forth from the womb,
> when I made the clouds its garment
>   and wrapped it in thick darkness,
> when I fixed limits for it
>   and set its doors and bars in place,
> when I said, 'This far you may come and
>   no farther;
> here is where your proud waves halt' . . .
>
> Can you bind the beautiful Pleiades?
>   Can you loose the cords of Orion?
> Can you bring forth the constellations in their seasons
>   or lead out the Bear with its cubs?
> Do you know the laws of the heavens?
>   Can you set up God's dominion over the earth?
>   (Job 38:8–11; 31–33).

When Jesus came striding across the pages of history, he reiterated the challenge: look carefully at the birds, contemplate the lilies, (Matt. 6:26, 28); an extraordinary invitation for a bunch of uncouth fishermen. But Paul explains why God persists in this way. God's invisible qualities are made visible through the things which he creates. His power and majesty and mystery are encapsulated in some measure in the work of his hands (Rom. 1:20).

The mystics learned to read this visible language. Take St Anthony for example. To his hermitage in the desert came one of the wise men of the time who said, 'How can you endure to live here, deprived as you are of all consolation from books?' Anthony replied, 'My book, philosopher, is the nature of created things, and, whenever I wish, I can read in it the works of God.'[2]

Brother Lawrence glories in the changing seasons which speak to him of the constancy of God.[3] And Prince Vladimir Monomakh of Kiev writes in similar vein: 'See how the sky, the sun and moon and stars, the darkness and the light, and the earth that is laid upon the waters, are ordered, O Lord, by thy providence! See how the different animals, and the birds and fishes, are adorned through thy loving care, O Lord!'[4]

When, one day, I read Carlo Carretto's invitation: 'Contemplate what lies before you. It is God's way of making himself present.' I was conscious of a restlessness within. This was exactly what I ached to do but I was not sure how to go about it. Yes. I could look at a purple anemone, wonder at its velvet petals, feel its texture, touch its tough stem and that small flower in my hands would bring me to the threshold of the mystery of the God who could manufacture such intricacies, but I sensed there was something more to contemplating the creativity of God.

By this time, a small group in my church had joined me in my quest to listen to God more effectively. They were as anxious as I was to plumb the depths of the parables of nature, to use the language of Carlo Carretto, so we decided to devote one Saturday to learning this art. Stephen Verney, the Bishop of Repton, agreed to introduce us to a form of meditation which many people of prayer use in an attempt to hear God speaking through very ordinary objects: a flower, a tree, a telegraph post.

I recall the Saturday well. The sun shone on the Derbyshire hills which encircle the bishop's house. The hedgerows and meadows were studded with wild flowers: harebells, buttercups, meadow-sweet, cowslips. We stood on the terrace of the bishop's home, drank coffee, and drank in, too, the magnificence of the countryside in summer. Then we went inside.

As we sat in a circle in the lounge, the bishop invited us to focus our attention on a bowl of wild flowers on a small table in the centre of the circle. 'Just waste time looking at them,' he invited. After a few minutes he turned to Matthew 6 and read Jesus's command: 'Consider the lilies...'. 'This word "consider" really means "contemplate",' the bishop suggested. 'When we contemplate something, we look at it from many angles, we touch it, feel it, smell it and learn from it. That is what I propose we do this morning.'

He passed the bowl of flowers round the room and invited each person to choose one. 'Now let's first spend time contemplating the flower we have chosen,' he said.

I had chosen a marguerite, the kind of big, wild daisy I love to watch waving in the breeze on a summer's day. But I had never looked at one so closely before. I gazed at its golden eye and felt its flimsy, fur-like petals. I squeezed its firm stem and turned it over to examine the pinkish underside.

The bishop's voice broke in on my contemplation: 'What is God saying through this flower?' he asked. The words which came to me immediately were simple and straightforward: 'I made that,' God seemed to say. I thought about that statement for several minutes. When my children or friends make something with their own hands, I treasure it. This common marguerite, the kind I trampled on in the fields every time I went for a walk in summer, was a portion of God's creativity. A treasure. An expression of his personality.

The bishop's voice filtered into my consciousness again: 'What is God saying to *you* through this flower?' he was asking.

I fingered the flower lovingly, respecting it now because of the one who manufactured it. And a verse from the Psalms imprinted itself on my mind:

> I praise you because I am fearfully and
>   wonderfully made;
> your works are wonderful,
> I know that full well (Ps. 139:14).

The flower, I could see, was fearfully and wonderfully designed by the master-craftsman of the world. I marvelled at his handiwork.

'Now I'd like to invite you to imagine how it would feel to *become* that flower.' The Bishop's voice interrupted my train of thought once more.

At first I thought it sounded a silly idea to try to *become* a flower. But I respected Stephen Verney and knew him to be a man who had ventured much further along the path of prayer than I had, and in doing so had gained the experience I coveted, so I decided to lay aside my pride and try to 'become' a marguerite.

To my surprise it was easy. I identified all too readily with the feelings a marguerite might feel if it were sentient: the vulnerability of being plucked from its moorings, sorrow at the violence of man whose greed demands that he possess the beauty he sees, emptiness at being removed so suddenly from the sustenance nature normally supplied.

'What is God saying to you now?'

The verse from Psalm 139 which had already been engraved on my heart, returned with fresh force. Through it, God seemed to show me that, though at times, I am as vulnerable and frail and helpless and misused as the marguerite, I am still a part of his creation, uniquely designed, the object of his care, cherished.

This reassurance brought a rich measure of healing that day. Assured that I was cherished by God, I reached out to him and opened myself to the energy which he longs should pulsate through our bodies, minds and spirits.

'I'd like you now to imagine yourself surrounded by your relatives and colleagues and friends,' the bishop said. 'Imagine that they are standing around you in a semi-circle. Picture them. Name them. Ask God to show you how you can convey to them the riches which he has given to you this morning.'

I thought of my husband, my two children, certain members of the church and my neighbours. I asked God to show me practical ways in which I could offer them his love. I was amused to discover how down-to-earth some of the suggestions seemed to be: 'You'll have been away for the whole day; express your thanks by cooking them a favourite meal!' I thought of one person I was counselling at the time. She needed to hear what I had heard from God: that she was valued by God and would be sustained by him. I prayed that I might communicate this message to her in a way she could imbibe.

Before we parted, the bishop invited us to turn to the person next to us and to attempt to explain what we had learned from God through the flower. When I voiced what I had experienced, it underlined the truths which God had been imparting. As I spelt out these truths my gratitude grew.

At first I kept this kind of meditation for my structured times of quiet with God. But some months after this group Quiet Day, a poem inspired me to look for God in this way anywhere and everywhere:

I hear you
   in the cry of the gull
   in the wind chasing the last leaves of fall
   in the whisper of a child

I see you
   in the animal shapes of cumulus clouds
   in the trees ten times my age
   in the wrinkled face of a woman over ninety . . .

I touch you
   in the smooth bark of a white birch
   in the rock beneath the summit tearing my hands
   in the texture of wet and dry sand.[5]

This poem pushed me into walking around with my eyes and ears open. I would be walking in the Derbyshire hills watching the sunset. God would speak to me of his majesty as he splashed the sky with golds and reds. Again, God would speak as I watched the clematis buds tilt their faces to the spring sun. I became acutely aware that everything God made pulsates with his uncreated energy; all things are sustained by him and, in one sense, are a theophany. Whether I was walking or sitting on the beach or in the garden or travelling in the bus, I would meditate on God's world, asking myself:

* What is God saying through this scene or object?

* What is he saying to *me*?

* What happens when I become that object?

* How can I take what I have learned into my world?

Just before starting to write this chapter, I wandered through the woodland walks in the rhododendron gardens near my home. At the moment they blaze with colour: pinks, vermilions, sherbet-lemon yellows, purples, creams, whites. As I gazed at such extravagance it was as though I was being embraced by God. When I walked into the gardens it seemed as though God greeted me, as though he had been searching for me and was glad that I had come. When I stretched out my hand to touch this beauty, I became aware that I touched a beauty which is part of him. The music of this visual harmony had been composed by him. The boundless ever-newness of this extravaganza leaves me spell-bound. But as I contemplate his creativity I catch, too, a glimpse of his glory.

As I learned to welcome him more and more, to hear him speak through the language of his world, I was introduced to the mystery of God in a new way. The mystery is that God is not so much the object of our knowledge as the cause of our wonder. The mystery is that I shall never know God exhaustively yet I may know sufficient to feel compelled to fall at his feet in wonder, love and praise. The mystery is that he is both hidden and revealed. The mystery is that he reveals his greatness through everyday objects: in the teaching of Jesus, through the coin which the woman had lost, through the yeast which caused her bread to rise, through the children who played in the market square and in the annals of Jeremiah, through the potter who shaped and re-shaped his clay.

On more than one occasion, God trickled healing, holding love into my grazed emotions through contemplating such ordinary objects.

It was September and, as is my custom, I had prepared a bowl of potting compost, buried a hyacinth bulb in it and thrust it into a deep, dark cupboard. While I was attempting to pray later that day, God seemed to give me a glimpse of the activity which would soon cause that bulb to change: the white roots which would push their way out of the shrivelled up bulb and into the nourishing soil; the green poker-like shoot which would nudge its way above the surface of the earth; the tiny flowers which would unfold and, in bursting open, would fill my study with fragrance.

I was suffering from a prolonged and painful bout of depression at the time. When the voice which I was learning to recognise as God's whispered, 'This is what the darkness of depression will do for you; it will result, eventually, in prolific growth and wholeness,' I felt strangely comforted. When the depression did its worst, it was to this visual promise that I clung.

It has never worried me that this kind of meditation leans heavily on the use of the imagination. I came across a phrase which C. S. Lewis uses, 'the baptised imagination', and this encouraged me to believe that when our imagination is soaked in the living waters of the Holy Spirit, God can use it. Similarly, John Powell makes the claim: 'God has access to us through the power of imagination.' He quotes a short excerpt from George Bernard Shaw's play, *St Joan:*

Robert: How do you mean? voices?

Joan: I can hear voices telling me what to do. They come from God.

Robert: They come from your imagination.

Joan: Of course. That is how the messages of God come to us.[6]

I, too, firmly believe that when the imagination is handed over to God, it is a powerful tool in the hand of a God who seeks to communicate his message of healing love through a whole variety of ways.

And the fear of pantheism, which keeps many Christians from hearing God speak through nature, does not trouble me either. I am clear in my mind that when I claim to hear God speak through the lips of a tulip, he speaks, not because he *is* the tulip, but because, as the creator of the tulip, he is giving expression to facets of himself through its design, its texture, its shape, its size and the streaks of red which he paints on the yellow petals with one stroke of his brush.

As my experience of listening to God through nature increased, I echoed the assurance of St Symeon:

> I know the Immovable comes down:
> I know the Invisible appears to me;
> I know that he who is far outside the whole creation,
> Takes me within himself and hides me in his arms . . .[7]

Chapter 12

How God Speaks: Tongues, Prophecy, Words of Wisdom and Knowledge

I was greedy, always thirsting for the 'something more' which God delights to give to his children. I took to heart the advice of St Isaac the Syrian which I had read: 'Thirst after Jesus and he will satisfy you with his love.'[1]

As I read the teaching Paul gave to the Corinthian Christians on listening to God, I recognised that there were yet more lessons to be learned:

> Now to each one the manifestation of the Spirit is given for the common good. To one there is given through the Spirit the message of wisdom, to another the message of knowledge by means of the same Spirit, to another... prophecy... to another speaking in different kinds of tongues, and to still another the interpretation of tongues (1 Cor. 12:7–10).

I smiled as I read those verses and recalled the days when I feared the gift of tongues. Even when God had taken me by surprise and overwhelmed me with his Holy Spirit's life and joy, I insisted that I would never speak in tongues.

Now that I viewed prayer as a developing friendship with God, this gift of the Spirit was no longer something I despised. It was something I valued. I saw it as a love-language with which I could express the adoration which sometimes burned in my heart when I worshipped God. I saw it as a means of expressing the spontaneous praise which sometimes leapt from the inner recesses of my being rather like the jet of a giant fountain. I saw it as a method of communicating to God the wonder, love and awe I felt, which even the Psalms could not adequately put into words.

As I became less embarrassed about this supernatural language, I would use it sometimes when praying with people who had come to me for counselling. From time to time this would give birth to an interpretation which would speak incisively to the situation we had been discussing or which would bring immediate and profound comfort and peace to a person in distress.

If tongues could contribute to my personal prayer life and benefit others, I felt sure that the other pieces of God's grammar and syntax which Paul mentions here must have equal value. But so far, I knew little about the supernatural gifts of wisdom, knowledge and prophecy, so I set myself the task of discovering what these terms meant and whether I could expect God to speak to me in this way.

The Word of Wisdom

David Watson's book, *One in the Spirit*, had already dispelled many of the irrational and childish fears which had prejudiced me against the work of the Holy Spirit and, in particular, the gift of tongues. So I decided to refer to this book again. In it David Watson suggests that the word of wisdom is the God-given ability to speak an appropriate word on every occasion, to make the right decisions, to discern between good and evil. He reminds us of the remarkable demonstration of this gift recorded in 1 Kings 3:16-28. Two women approached Solomon and brought with them two babies. One was alive. The other dead. Each mother insisted that the living baby was *her* baby. Solomon, exercising the gift of wisdom, proposed slicing the live baby in two so that both mothers could keep one half. This elicited a protest from the real mother. She refused him permission to murder her child, thus revealing her true identity. The bogus mother would have been content to watch the baby being butchered.

Solomon had prayed for this gift of wisdom: 'O Lord my God, you have made your servant king in place of my father David. But I am only a little child and do not know how to carry out my duties ... So give your servant a discerning heart to govern your people and to distinguish between right and wrong' (1 Kgs. 3:7–9).

Solomon's prayer brought joy to God. As I meditated on it and the dynamic way in which God answered it, it stirred up in me a heart-hunger. I, too, longed to rely, not simply on skills which I had learned and acquired through experience, but on *God's* wisdom. This, I sensed, could transform my counselling ministry. In his epistle James encourages us to ask God to invest his wisdom in us. So I made my request.

Meanwhile, I stumbled on an amusing contemporary illustration of this gift in Keith Miller's challenging book, *The Taste of New Wine*.

One of the battlegrounds which troubled Keith Miller's marriage in the early days, it seems, was the conflict which erupted over role delineation. When they married, Mary Allen, his wife, assumed that he would empty the pedal bin in the kitchen each day. He, meanwhile, felt insulted by the suggestion. This was woman's work in his view. He refused to capitulate to his wife's demands.

After his conversion to Christ, Keith Miller tried to convince his wife that he had found something wonderful in God, that God was changing her husband's personality. In an attempt to convince her of the strength of this claim he looked for ways of demonstrating this truth by his behaviour.

He goes on to explain how the word of wisdom flashed into his awareness: 'While I was looking around for some... way to convince my wife that I had really changed, my glance fell on the waste basket standing full by the back door. "No, Lord," I groaned quietly to myself. "*Not* the waste basket. Take my income, anything." '[2]

After a struggle, he obeyed. He emptied the waste basket. 'Without saying a word I took it out, and didn't even mention it to her.'

Mary Allen, of course, took note of this change in attitude. She continued to refuse her husband's invitations to Christian meetings but she did begin to ask a friend penetrating questions about the Christian faith. These discussions resulted, in time, in her own conversion to Christianity. When she retraced the way God had wooed her to himself she recognised that her husband's gesture that day he emptied the waste basket had been one of the prongs God had used to prod her in his direction.

Situations like these taught me that the word of wisdom, God's incisive word given for a specific occasion, comes winged with power and authenticity. Often it comes laced with humour also.

The word of knowledge

I was to learn that, just as God grants a person the gift of wisdom, so he speaks powerfully, precisely and economically through words of knowledge. A word of knowledge is an insight implanted by God about a particular person or situation for a specific purpose. Alex Buchanan, in a talk given to our fellowship on one occasion, summarised the gift helpfully:

The word of knowledge may be the revelation of the whereabouts or the doings of a man, the nature of his thought, or the condition of his heart. It is a gift of revelation. It becomes vocal when shared with others. It is a fragment of divine knowledge which cannot be attained by study or consecration. It is a divinely granted flash of revelation concerning things which were hopelessly hidden from the senses, the mind, or the faculties of men.

I was to discover that Jesus exercised this gift. His use of it astounded the Samaritan woman who talked with him at the well. Although Jesus had never encountered this woman before, so far as we know, he seemed well informed about her sex life. 'You have had five husbands, and the man you now have is not your husband' (John 4:18). This word of knowledge not only astonished this woman, it resulted in a complete change of life-style.

I found Jesus exercising this gift again after the Resurrection. The disciples were fishing on the Sea of Galilee. Although the lake normally teemed with fish, on this trip, they caught nothing. Jesus called to them from the shore: 'Throw your net on the right side of the boat and you will find some.' John records the result of the disciples' obedience to this word of knowledge: 'When they did, they were unable to haul the net in because of the large number of fish' (John 21:6).

God still speaks, convicts and consoles through these flashes of inspiration. The first time God spoke to me in this way I was both startled and amused.

My husband and I were house-parents at a houseparty for students and, during the course of the conference, I had spoken on boy/girl relationships and on prayer.

One evening, a young man asked if he could talk to me. He told me that his prayer life was dry and arid, that when he prayed his words seemed to hit the ceiling and bounce back at him like a boomerang. I listened and we talked about his prayer life for nearly half an hour but somehow I realised we were not really communicating. Without warning, and for no other reason than the prompting of the Holy Spirit, the word 'masturbation' lodged in my brain. At first I tried to push it away. But the voice within refused to be silenced. 'His prayer problem is a guilt problem. He's feeling guilty about a masturbatory problem,' the voice insisted.

Feeling rather nervous and foolish, I steered the conversation away from prayer *per se* and on to the subject of guilt. The young man blushed and then started talking about 'his besetting sin'. When eventually I mentioned the word masturbation he sighed with relief and real communication began.

Left to rely on my own insights, I would have failed utterly to make a direct connection between prayer and masturbation. On that occasion, and on many subsequent occasions, I have thanked God for the time-saving inner prompting of the gift of knowledge. It does not replace counselling skills or sensitivity or the need for solidarity with a person's pain. But it is a valuable tool with which God equips us as we seek to bring people to wholeness.

This gift is not for super-saints. It is for everyone. If we are open to God, he uses it, not only in the way I have described above, but to nudge us into prayer and action when and where prayer is specially needed.

I had written one third of this chapter of this book when I decided to take a coffee break. As I filled the kettle with water, the name of a friend popped into my mind and I sensed this person needed my prayers. There in the kitchen, I lifted him into the all-loving hands of God. Two minutes later, the phone rang. I should not have been surprised to hear this friend's voice at the end of the phone: 'Will you pray for me please?' he said. 'I'm off work today and I've just come back from the doctor. It's suspected appendicitis.'

That kind of connecting happens so regularly now that I am no longer tempted to believe it is mere coincidence. I take such promptings as God's promptings and try to act on them appropriately.

Prophecy
Another discovery I made is that words of wisdom, knowledge and prophecy intertwine and overlap with one

another. David Watson described prophecy in this way: 'Prophecy is a message from God, which is not necessarily anything to do with the future: a forth-telling not primarily a foretelling... It is a word from the Lord through a member of the body of Christ, inspired by the Spirit, to build up the rest of the body' (1 Cor. 14:3-5).[3]

Alex Buchanan helped me enormously as I sought to understand this gift. He suggests that this gift as we have it in the church today finds three expressions. There is 'low level prophecy', where God might encourage a person or a congregation with a simple statement: 'The Lord says: "Don't be afraid. I am with you." ' There is a 'higher level' of prophecy where God reveals something about the situation in a particular church at a particular time. And there is the 'highest level' of prophecy which causes people to bow down and worship God in awe and wonder because they know, 'The Lord has spoken.'

I noticed that Paul exhorts us to 'eagerly desire spiritual gifts, especially the gift of prophecy... everyone who prophesies speaks to men for their strengthening, encouragement and comfort' (1 Cor. 14:1,3). And so I became covetous for this gift too.

On one occasion, at a student conference where I was speaking, one of the other speakers gave a word of prophecy which would fall into Alex Buchanan's third category: the highest level of prophecy. The speaker spelt out the vision of God which he could see in his mind's eye. It was reminiscent of parts of the book of Revelation or of Isaiah's vision of God. We, the listeners, were scarcely conscious of the words. Jesus filled our entire horizon. When the words stopped, a powerful hush silenced the group, a silence pregnant with worship, adoration and wordless praise. God had spoken, to strengthen, encourage and uplift us. I was left in no doubt that God still speaks in this way today.

God also demonstrated to me that his use of prophecy to warn his church is as accurate, painful and uncomfortable as it was in Old Testament times.

I was invited to speak to a group of church leaders on one occasion but had been out of the country on sabbatical leave for four months, so knew little of what had been going on in that church in recent weeks. While I was preparing for the conference, a sense of heaviness overwhelmed me. I quote from the notes I made as I listened to God for that occasion: 'There are some leaders here who are battle-scarred, weary, resourceless from over-much pouring out. There are others who are blatantly disobedient. Unless their life-style changes, they will be weeded out of leadership by our Lord himself. He will not use dirty vessels.'

I felt extremely vulnerable as I gave this talk. What if I was wrong? What if *God* had not revealed these things . . . ?

Within a year, five leaders had resigned, unable to cope with the pressures of family, responsible jobs and leadership in the church; several key people had resigned because they were committing gross sexual sin.

At this time, a member of that congregation was given a word of prophecy for the church which she offered with hesitancy and an open-ness to be corrected. The prophecy reads: 'I am raising up the debris of society to take the leadership you will not take. Those you count as nothing. . . who know their need and acknowledge their dependence on me, will overtake you and leave you as nothing.'

Today, former leaders in that church have fallen away. A whole new leadership is emerging. It consists of many unlikely people. The prophecy, it seems, is being fulfilled.

As I looked more closely at the gift of prophecy, I saw that if a prophetic word is from God, it will edify or exhort or comfort (see 1 Cor. 14:31). It will not necessarily be painless. Indeed, it will cut into a situation and cause pain, even fear. This is not unlike the incision the surgeon makes with his scalpel. It is the pain which precedes purging and healing, which is, in fact, an act of love.

The prophetic word is not only a word of love; it is also a timely word in the sense that it is necessary for that person or that group of people at that particular time. It is also an accurate word. Its accuracy survives the test of time. If it originates in God, the minutest details will be fulfilled.

On the day of Pentecost, as we have already seen, Peter quoted Joel's prophecy:

> In the last days, God says,
> I will pour out my Spirit on all people.
> Your sons and daughters will prophesy,
>   your young men will see visions,
> Your old men will dream dreams.
> Even on my servants, both men and women,
> I will pour out my Spirit in those days,
>   and they will prophesy (Acts 2:17,
>   quoting Joel 2:28–32).

I began to realise that we live in those exciting 'last days'. And I began to realise that Christians who open themselves to the Holy Spirit of God will, as occasion demands, be entrusted with the supernatural gifts of wisdom and knowledge, prophecy and visions. I would now go further. Like David Watson, I recognise that these gifts are 'tremendously important for every age'. They are 'not made redundant by the completion of the God-given revelation in the scriptures.'[4] Rather, they are made available for us by God through the anointing of his Holy Spirit.

God speaks through very ordinary, everyday events and objects. And God speaks through the supernatural. That God speaks at all today still sent a shiver of anticipation down my spine whenever I turned to prayer. I expected God to speak. And he did.

Chapter 13

Many Mistakes

Listening to God is not always as straightforward as it seems. At least, this is my experience. At times it can even seem quite frightening.

I am a person who likes to keep at least one toe on the ground while swimming in the sea. Similarly, I like to keep well within my depth in a spiritual sense. But there were times when the tide seemed to sweep me along with it and I was forced to respond to the challenge to become a stronger swimmer.

The problem was that although I knew that God speaks today and that his messages are transmitted in a multitude of ways and although I had experienced the fact that he wants to gain *my* attention, to communicate to me, I was also becoming increasingly aware that the pictures I saw, the dreams I dreamed, and the inner voice I heard did not always originate in God. If my suspicion was correct, then where did these phenomena spring from? And how was I supposed to discern the real from the spurious?

One night, for example, a vivid dream startled me. My husband and I were on holiday in Austria at the time. David is a keen photographer and, like a mountain goat, he will sometimes leap to seemingly precarious places in order to 'get a better shot'. In my dream, David and I were walking in the mountains in the way we love to do. Suddenly a breath-taking scene of snow-capped mountain cones framed by an expanse of cornflower blue sky opened up before us. David edged himself on to a wobbly ledge to capture the scene on film when, all of a sudden, he fell. At first, fear paralysed me. But then it propelled me into action. I ran and ran as fast as I could until I reached the spot where he lay. But I was too late. His body was slumped in a heap. He was dead.

Next morning, fear seemed to hold me in a vice-like grip. For some reason I cannot fathom even now, I was unable to voice this fear to David. Perhaps I was afraid that if I described the accident it might even happen? That evening we had a minor accident in the car. All that happened was that we demolished a bollard at the edge of the road but my nerves, still shattered by the vividness of the dream, gave way. Hysterical, I clung to David, sobbed, and poured out the details of the dream which was making me so miserable. The panic only subsided after we had prayed together.

On a previous holiday, God *had* spoken to me through the dream I described in an earlier chapter. Of that fact I was now convinced. But this dream clearly had not come from the same loving source. Where *had* it come from?

Some months later, David and I attended an interview for a new job. While I was praying on the day of the interview, I sensed God was telling me that we would be appointed to this new post. I was glad. I would enjoy a series of new challenges.

Three days after the interview, the expected phone call came but the voice at the other end did not give the anticipated message. On the contrary, it said: 'We'd like to thank David and yourself for giving up your time to attend the interview. I am sorry to tell you we are unable to offer you the job. Someone else is now considering the post. We will confirm this in a letter in a day or two.'

I placed the phone in its cradle and was relieved that the house was empty. The shock left me numbed. Had God not kept his promise? Impossible. Had the interviewers made a mistake? Unlikely. So many people had prayed about this appointment. Then I must have been mistaken in my listening. Listening to God was not as straightforward as I imagined.

Other people were having problems with separating the real from the spurious, too. I knew of this because some of them were honest enough to tell me.

There was the woman who said, 'The Lord has told me to write a book. I'm to write the story of my life.' She spent years writing her book but was unable to find a publisher. Had her listening been accurate? Had *God* told her to write the book?

There was the Christian student who confessed to me that he had been sleeping with his non-Christian girl-friend for several months. He told me that, since it would be impossible for them to marry for several years, but since they were committed to one another, God had told him it was permissible for them to have sexual intercourse. What did I think?

And there was the person who asked to see me because she was utterly confused. 'Joyce! I don't know what to do any more. You see, I keep hearing all these voices in my head telling me what to do. I think it's the Holy Spirit talking to me. I used to read my Bible regularly and do what it told me to do. But now I don't know which to believe. So I've stopped reading my Bible and just do what the Holy Spirit says.'

Without ever realising what they were doing, these people helped me to face up to the fact that those of us who embark on the adventure of listening to God are going to make mistakes. For listening to God can be the most sublime and joy-filled privilege in the world or it can become the most absurd exercise we ever embark on.

For sheer absurdity, I have never encountered an example which surpasses the one quoted by Jim Packer:

There was once a woman who sincerely wanted to listen

to God about the details of her life. Each morning, having consecrated the day to the Lord as she woke, she would then ask whether she was to get up or not. She would not stir until the still, small voice told her to dress. As she put on each article she asked the Lord whether she was to put it on. Very often the Lord would tell her to put her right shoe on but to leave the other off. Sometimes she was to put on both stockings but no shoes and sometimes both shoes and no stockings. And thus listening to God she would deal with every article of dress in turn.[1]

Mistakes! Mistakes! Mistakes! When I read stories like this, counselled people like the ones I have mentioned above and smarted over the situations I mishandled myself, there were times when I was tempted to abandon my quest. But a claim Thomas Merton makes in one of his books lodged in my mind and prevented me from abandoning all that I had learned to treasure. Thomas Merton says of mistakes that the only one which is really a mistake is that from which we learn nothing. I had also heard David Watson's maxim: 'The antidote to *abuse* is not *dis*use but *right* use.' In the light of these challenges I determined to allow a whole string of mistakes to become, not my censors, but my teachers.

Recognise the source

A talk given by Jean Darnall at a Swanwick conference I attended cleared away the mists of confusion which swirled round my brain and my emotions. 'Test the spirits,' she challenged. 'Make certain that what you are hearing comes from God.' She pointed us to the scriptures: 'Dear friends, do not believe every spirit, but test the spirits to see whether they are from God, because many false prophets have gone out into the world...' (1 John 4:1).

Later, when I followed this theme up for myself, I noticed that this solemn warning has been woven into the

fabric of the New Testament's teaching. Jesus warned us
to beware of the wolves who come to us in sheep's
clothing. Paul begs us not to quench the Spirit by putting
out his fire, nor to treat prophecy with contempt, but he
also urges us to 'Test everything. Hold on to the good.' (1
Thess. 5:19). In James, I found advice which further
clarified my own position: 'The wisdom that comes from
heaven is first of all pure; then peace-loving, considerate,
submissive, full of mercy and good fruit, impartial and
sincere' (Jas. 3:17).

When I applied this verse to my two dreams, I saw the
difference immediately. The one I dreamed in Greece
which had prepared me to face up to imminent tragedy
was 'peace-loving' in the sense that, horrifying though it
was, it left my heart and mind full of God's peace rather
than full of terror. The dream which interrupted my sleep
in Austria, on the other hand, was not only terrifying in its
attention to detail, but it left me panic-stricken. The lack
of peaceableness, had I known about this verse in James at
the time of the dream, could have been my clue. This
dream had not emanated from God.

Three possible sources

If my dream was not sent from God, where did it spring
from? Again, it was Jean Darnall who showed me that
dreams and visions and voices and thoughts come from
three possible sources:

* the Holy Spirit

* my own spirit

* the Evil One.

That made immediate sense. I reflected on my second
dream again and saw that it had not been prophetic but
simply an expression of my neurotic fear that David would
one day slip over the side of a precipice while taking

photographs. I laughed. The laughter brought a new perspective: of course the dream described my neurosis in technicolour detail. God would only feature in it if I were to hand the fear over to him.

I thought, too, of 'the word' which assured me that we would be appointed to the new post. Again, I smiled in a wry kind of way. How easy it was to listen to the voice of pride and wishful thinking and hang the Lord's name around their neck. I realised that I was still wearing L plates where listening to God is concerned. Probably I always will. As Thomas Merton observes: 'We do not want to be beginners. But let us be convinced of the fact that we will never be anything else but beginners all our life!'[2] For this reason I was grateful to Jean Darnall for the practical advice she gave me at that time. 'If you believe God has told you to do something,' she advised, 'ask him to confirm it to you three times: through his word, through circumstances, and through other people who may know nothing of the situation.'

For the next twelve months I became far more cautious about listening to God. I tested the ground in the way Jean suggested. And I was grateful for the apprenticeship, which enabled me to grow in confidence.

I now realise that we can never be one hundred per cent certain that the picture we see or the voice we hear or the prophecy we speak out is winged to us from God. That is why listening to God is hard, why speaking out in the name of God is costly and leaves us feeling vulnerable.

If the voice is truly from God, it will have an ice-cutting quality about it. Someone will hear it and say, 'Oh yes! I see!' If the voice comes from our own hurt spirit or over-anxious or over-loving spirit, no lasting harm will be done so we need not worry. But we shall be able to tell the difference between this and God's voice because there will be a lack of authority and dynamism about what is shared. The word or picture will probably fall flat on its face like a badly told joke.

But what if a word or a picture or a dream or an intuition is planted in one's heart by the Evil One? This seemed to me far-more serious and, I admit, the possibility worried me. Satan, I know, loves to fake spiritual gifts. He is skilled in the art of the counterfeit.

Know the Father-heart of God

While I was still worrying over this question, Alex Buchanan, whom I had first met when he was on the staff of St Michael-le-Belfrey Church, in York, and whose friendship my husband and I had grown to value, made one of those pronouncements whose divine origin one recognises immediately. On a visit to our home he said, 'If you want to be certain that you are truly listening to God, you must know the Father-heart of God.' I was glad that there were others in the room when he turned that statement into a question. 'Do you *know* the Father-heart of God?'

I knew what he meant by this question. He was asking whether we knew the mind of God, whether we understood the personality of God, whether we were acquainted with the will of God and the way he normally acts and reacts in certain situations. He was asking whether we were familiar with the pronouncements God has made on certain subjects. He made it clear that the way to distinguish between God's voice and Satan's voice was to become acquainted with what lay in God's Father-heart.

That made sense to me. That very week I had taken a phone call for David which had demonstrated to me the value of knowing someone's mind in this intuitive way. A friend had telephoned one evening and asked to speak to my husband. David was out. 'Oh well, Joyce, you'll do,' the voice said. 'I was going to ask whether he would be interested in a new job. I'd like to put his name forward if I may.'

'Well,' I replied, 'I'm ninety-nine per cent certain that

David would say that at the moment he feels God is asking us to stay in Nottingham.'

When David came home, I asked him, 'If someone was to ask if they could put your name forward for a new job, what would you say?'

David used almost the same words I had used earlier: 'I'd say that I feel that we're being asked to stay in Nottingham at the moment.'

I live with David. We have spent years working at the art of communication. I know his mind. I know his personality. I know his plans. I talk to him and I listen to him. Was it possible to know God in this intuitive way also?

I was preparing to preach a sermon on Daniel at the time. Daniel seemed conversant with the Father-heart of God. Daniel offered me the master key. It came in the form of a pithy observation: 'I, Daniel understood from the scriptures...' (Dan. 9:2). To understand means here: to consider in detail, to go through carefully, to examine, to scrutinise. Daniel knew the Father-heart of God because Daniel applied his *mind* to the hard work of understanding God's Word so that he could understand God himself.

The psalmist was another man whose writings reflect an intimate knowledge of God. When I searched for his secret, I discovered his, too, was an open secret. David familiarised himself with the Father-heart of God by familiarising himself with scripture. David delighted in God's Word, treasured it, steeped himself in it, respected it, memorised it, pored over it, examined it and determined never to veer from it.[3] He meditated on God's revealed word day and night and exhorted others to follow his example (Ps. 1:2).

That these men built a close relationship with God because they applied their energies and time and minds to the study of God's Word came as a sharp and salutary reminder. God seemed to be warning me again that listening to him is not just a matter of openness or willingness to hear his still, small voice. It is not just a matter of meditating, internalising the message or contemplating him, it is also a matter of hard work and application. When listening to God, inspiration and perspiration walk hand in hand.

God gave this same warning through John Wesley: 'Do not ascribe to God what is not of God. Do not easily suppose dreams, voices, impressions, visions, revelations to be from God without sufficient evidence. They may be purely natural, they may be diabolical. Try all things by the written Word and let all bow down before it.'

If my student friend had done this, I reflected, there would have been no need to ask my advice about his relationship with his girl-friend. The Bible makes it quite clear that to be unequally yoked with an unbeliever is to accept second best in marriage, not God's best. The Bible also makes it clear that sexual intercourse has one context and one context only: marriage. Any voice which tells an unmarried person that they are absolved from this clear biblical teaching must therefore be rejected. It is not God's voice. God will not contradict himself. God's truth is not negotiable.

Similarly, I thought of my friend who had abandoned Bible reading in favour of listening to the voices in her head. I understood now why anger had burned inside me when she told me of her decision. I had not been angry against her but against that serpent, Satan, who still bewitches us and uses all and every means to side-track us from the narrow path which leads to life.

There could be no finger pointing on my part. I was too busy making my own mistakes and learning from them to have time to wage war against others. But I knew that in future I must test my listening by asking four questions:

* Is the result of this piece of listening in alignment with scripture?

* Do the circumstances substantiate what I heard? Has it come true?

* Is my attitude Christ-like, characterised by humility, or is it reminiscent of Satan, the rebellious one?

* Is this still, small voice prompting me or others to live in a way which honours God and obeys him, or will the suggestion bring his name and honour into question or disrepute?

As I pondered on these criteria for accurate listening, I recognised that here was a charge from God. If I am to listen to God for married people in trouble, as I do, I must first know what God's Word says about marriage. If I am to help unmarried people with sexual problems, as I do, I owe it to them to be certain what lies in the Father-heart of God concerning their problems and their person.

God had challenged me. However fascinated I became with his presence, his power and his ability to communicate, I must not allow my knowledge of the scriptures to grow rusty. At the same time, I took comfort from Francis Schaeffer's reassuring observation. Speaking of people who steep themselves in the gospel, maintain a high view of scripture *and* give a proper emphasis to God's Spirit he maintains that God will use them even if they make mistakes, as undoubtedly they will: 'If we preach the gospel clearly, have a strong view of scripture with a strong emphasis on content and give adequate place to the Holy Spirit, God will use us even if we make mistakes - and, I repeat, none of us are free from mistakes.'[4]

Use your intelligence

Even so, I wanted to avoid making mistakes wherever possible. To speak in the name of Christ must not be done lightly. Mistakes must be taken seriously. Since it was becoming clear that my fallibility could cloud God's clarity, I determined to take on board two other suggestions which God seemed to underline. First is the need to submit what I hear to others so that they can weigh the word or picture language, sift it and determine its origin. Second is the responsibility I have not to neglect my intellect but to sharpen my powers of thinking. I took seriously a warning given by no less a listener than St John of the Cross who says on several occasions that we should not demand supernatural intervention when we are capable of understanding a situation for ourselves. God gave us our intellect to be used and used to the full. When the light of my own human intelligence is sufficient for the task in hand, he will not superimpose on it spiritual enlightenment. I thought of Jim Packer's story of the woman who waited for God to tell her what to wear, and asked to be delivered from the laziness which masquerades for a super-spirituality. And I resolved to become, to use the language of John Wesley, *uniùs homo libri*, a person of one book, the Bible.

Chapter 14

The Bible: the Touchstone of Listening

In all our listening, the most penetrating word we shall ever hear is God's written Word, the Bible, that sword which slips into the inner recesses of our being, challenging us, changing us, and renewing our minds. As we saw in the previous chapter, those who urge us to steep ourselves in the scriptures bring a vital, indispensable emphasis to the art form of listening prayer. The Bible is the touchstone of all our other listening. What is more, it has a power all its own.

J. B. Phillips testified to the power of this Word which springs from the Spirit of God. While he was translating the New Testament he discovered that God's Word was moulding his thinking: 'Although I did my utmost to preserve an emotional detachment, I found again and again that the material under my hands was strangely alive; it spoke to my condition in the most uncanny way.'[1]

Campbell McAlpine claims that this book, the Bible, 'is the *living word* of the *living God*'.[2] And Jesus lived by this Word. Moreover, he anticipated that the lives of believers would be shaped by it. He expected that all theological thinking would be tested in the light of his Father's 'letters from home', to borrow St Augustine's phrase. Thus when the Pharisees quizzed him about the marriage relationship, Jesus referred them to first biblical principles: 'Haven't you read . . . that at the beginning the Creator "made them male and female", and said, 'For this reason a man will leave his father and mother and be united to his wife, and the two will become one flesh?' (Matt. 19:4;5, quoting Gen. 2:24).

Jesus assumed his followers would possess a thorough working knowledge of the scriptures. When lack of biblical insight blinded their eyes, Jesus rebuked them. So, on the road to Emmaus, Jesus found fault with his ignorant companions: 'How foolish you are, and how slow of heart to believe all that the prophets have spoken! Did not the Christ have to suffer these things and then enter his glory? And beginning with Moses and all the prophets, he explained to them what was said in all the scriptures concerning himself' (Luke 24:25–27).

In the view of Jesus, it seems, the written Word contained in scripture is the Word of God. Jesus expresses this dramatically when, in the desert, he confronts Satan face to face. With authority and poise, he withstands the Enemy with one economical phrase: 'It is written...' (Luke 4:4,8).

For Jesus, as Jim Packer reminds us, 'It is written' was the end of the argument. 'There could be no appeal against the verdict of scripture for that would be to appeal against the judgement of God himself.'[3] For Jesus, the Old Testament taught and expressed God's mind and will. For this reason scripture was to be heeded, heard and obeyed. David Watson underlines these facts powerfully: 'The Bible is our final court of appeal for what God has said. Here is the God-given objective test for our belief and behaviour.'[4]

If I was to learn to listen to God accurately, to avoid the trap of tuning into my own emotions and mistaking these or wishful thinking for the voice of God, I knew it was incumbent on me to take these solemn words seriously. I must make time for Bible study.

Bible Study

In one sense this was not difficult. As a theology student who also read history and loved English literature, I learned to enjoy studying the Bible: Paul's epistles, the prophets, the historical books, the poetry and, of course, the gospels. I owe this enjoyment of the discipline of Bible study chiefly to my scripture teacher at school. A committed Christian who clearly relished God's Word herself, she passed on to me the desire to understand the written Word of God as well as the longing to interpret it accurately and to allow it to direct and renew my perception of life.

As an undergraduate, I sat at the feet of scholars whose love and respect for God's Word was equally profound. As I listened to them expound portions of scripture, like the psalmist, I delighted in God's revealed Word and felt nourished by it. In those days I never tired of the daily diet of Bible study.

When the demands of motherhood crept up on me, I grew lazy, even sloppy, in my attitude to the Bible. Although I struggled to have a Quiet Time most days and athough this would include the reading of a portion of scripture and a cursory glance at some Bible reading notes, I could scarcely claim that Bible *study* featured in my life. But now, with this insatiable thirst to unearth methods of listening to God, I made Bible study a priority once more. God's word would give me the objective, scientific, revealed framework into which the prophecies and visions would fit if they were born of him.

For a while, I studied the Bible every day. I applied myself to it with diligence. I analysed it, concentrated on it, sought to understand what the original author intended to communicate when he wrote what he did, then sought to understand why God had left us with this particular message for all time. I tried, equally, to apply what I read to my own circumstances. And I dug deep. When I came across commands which now seem obsolete because the structure of society has changed here in the West ('Slaves, obey your masters'), I used my thinking powers to try to ascertain what the lasting underlying principles of such commands might be. I wanted to be an *informed* Christian.

I rejoiced to be grafted back into God's Word. I remember shutting myself in my study one Saturday, littering my desk and floor with Bibles and commentaries, and concentrating on Psalm 119 for the entire day. By evening I was euphoric. Not only had God given me a special love for that psalm, with its one hundred and seventy-six verses, but I could re-echo much of it.

Oh, that my ways were steadfast in obeying your decrees! (9).

My soul is consumed with longing for your laws at all times (20).

Turn my heart towards your statutes and not towards selfish gain (36).

As I write this chapter Bible study is still, for me, a joyful privilege. I have just returned from two weeks away from home. While I was away on a retreat-holiday, I immersed myself in the first book of Kings. It is years since I read about the decline and fall of Israel and the spiritual downfall of Solomon and his successors to the throne. But through this application of my mind to his revealed Word, God reminded me of some salutary truths: enthusiasm for him is not enough, wisdom is not enough, fame is not enough; obedience to him is crucial for the person intent on progressing in the Christian life.

It is not only solo study which thrills me. Whenever I have the opportunity to attend Bible readings given by those gifted by God to present God's revealed Word in a systematic, scholarly way, I find my love for God rekindled. I crave for the richness of this diet. And it reminds me of the salient truth that God speaks to us first and foremost through our minds. No matter how skilled we become in tuning in to his multi-level methods of communication – 'hearing' prophecies and dreams and visions and 'vibes' – the starting point and check-point must always be God's Word revealed in the pages of the Bible. Unless we know what this Word contains we can never discern whether what we hear runs counter to the Bible and must therefore be discounted since God will not contradict himself.

Because Bible study has come to be of such importance in my listening prayer, it no longer features in my daily devotional time. I consider it too crucial for that. When a project becomes vital to my way of life, I carve out priority time for it. So, no matter how busy my schedule, I reserve quality time to spend with certain people, like my husband. Similarly, having recognised that Bible study is an indispensable part of listening to God, I create regular, leisurely opportunities when I can give myself to the commentaries and Bible dictionaries and the serious intellectual enquiry into the words which God has spoken and which are recorded for us for all time. I cannot concentrate on God's Word in this way on a *daily* basis, but I can commit myself to such study regularly.

Bible meditation

I am not saying I do not *read* the Bible every day. Most days I do. I am saying I do not study the Bible in an academic way each day. Instead I remind myself of God's truths by meditating on a portion of scripture.

My first introduction to this simple but profound method of Bible reading came through a book which boasts the simple title: *You.* I think I was attracted to the book by its sub-title: *Prayer for beginners and those who have forgotten how.* In it the author describes a reading technique which he calls 'super-slow reading'. Super-slow reading is reflective reading. You take a verse of scripture or a familiar passage and instead of studying it analytically, you read it as slowly as possible, presenting yourself to the situation described so forcibly that you begin to experience, with your imagination, the sights, sounds and feelings that are painted for you by the author.

The first time I experimented with this art of super-slow reading, Mark's account of the Crucifixion stunned me by its solemnity, then bruised my emotions with almost physical force:

> At the sixth hour
> darkness came over the whole land
> until the ninth hour.
> And at the ninth hour Jesus cried out in a loud voice,
> 'Eloi, Eloi, lama sabachthani?'
> which means,
> 'My God, my God, why have you forsaken me?'
> (Mark 15:33–34).

I knew those words so well I could probably have recited them without reference to the text. But as I practised super-slow reading, I pictured in my imagination the hill of Calvary where Jesus was strung up on his cross: Golgotha, the place of the skull. I could feel the intense heat of the mid-day sun burning his body. That phrase, 'darkness came over the whole land', terrified me as I saw the blackness descend like a blanket over the whole of Jerusalem and the surrounding countryside. The awfulness of that darkness sent a shudder right down my spine. It was my spine that reacted again as I heard the anguish of Jesus's shout pierce the gloom: 'My God, my God, why have you forsaken me?'

That day, I read these two verses from the gospel narrative and that was all. It was enough. This scene had changed my life. When you see Jesus writhing on the cross before your very eyes in the way I did that day, you have to make a personal response of humble, grateful surrender to such depths of loving.

For a while, I concentrated solely on this method of Bible reading. It transformed my attitude to the gospels. This was of particular value for me because I had attended Sunday School from the age of three. Consequently, I knew all the Jesus stories inside out (or I thought I did). Because I knew the punch-lines, the gospels had lost much of their drawing power. Paul's epistles held far more appeal than the accounts of Jesus's earthly pilgrimage. But super-slow reading changed all that.

So did another method of Bible reading which is attributed to St Ignatius of Loyola and is described by him in *Spiritual Exercises*. This method of reading the scriptures involves replaying in one's mind and heart a particular episode from the Bible. The idea behind the technique is that the reader relives the event which the gospel writer describes. Instead of standing on the fringe of the story as an observer, however, he becomes an active participant, immersing himself in what is happening and experiencing for himself with each of his five senses every detail of the story.

In other words, instead of simply reading about the woman who stretched out her hand to touch the hem of Jesus's garment, you *become* that woman and take the personal risk of reaching out to touch him. Instead of merely reading about the paralysed man who sat helplessly beside the pool of Bethesda, you *become* that man. You encounter Jesus for yourself. You talk to him. You hear his voice. You respond to his challenge: 'Do you want to get well?'

John Powell, in his book, *He Touched Me*, had encouraged me in the belief that God could speak through our five senses: sight, hearing, smell, taste and touch. This so-called Ignatian method of Bible reading convinced me of the authenticity of this claim.

Perhaps it is because God has endowed me with a vivid

and virile imagination that these meditations quickly became one of the ways God spoke to me. As I 'became' Mary, the mother of Jesus, sitting astride the back of a donkey on my way to visit Elizabeth, and as I pondered on the stupendous news Gabriel had just brought, 'You are to be the mother of the Messiah,' my heart leapt with joy at the sheer wonder of it all. Despite the intrusive noise I could hear – the clip-clop of the donkey's feet – praise rose from somewhere deep within me: 'My soul glorifies the Lord...'

In this meditation, I was not nursing grandiose opinions of myself, mistaking my mission, believing myself in reality to be the mother of Jesus. Rather, I was identifying with Mary as fully as my senses would allow in order that the Holy Spirit of God could break through with fresh insights. He did. The wonder of the Annunciation and the Incarnation: the Creator of the world lying in a cradle; God coming to be found and seen and touched by mankind, bowled me over with an impact a mere reading of the words had never done.

I began to write my own meditations and to use them personally. One Ascension time, in my imagination I climbed the Mount of Ascension with the disciples and watched Jesus's departure from earth using this guideline:

Imagine that you have been allowed the privilege of walking with the eleven, out of Jerusalem to the Mount of Ascension.

Stay behind them as you leave the noise and clutter and the stifling heat of Jerusalem behind.

Feel the heat warming your body as you start the steep climb.

Feel the warm dust creeping into your sandals.

What can you see...?

What can you hear...?

What can you smell...?

Take time to picture the whole scene as vividly as possible.

Become an integral part of it.

How do you feel?

Look at your companions, the eleven disciples.

What sort of people are they?

How are they dressed?

What are they talking about?

Is there anything you'd like to ask them – or say to them?

Now you are nearing the place where Jesus promised to meet you.

How does it feel to be about to meet him?

And now – there he is – standing in front of you!

How does it feel to see the risen Lord?

What do you want to do as you meet him?

Take a good look at Jesus –

    at those hands still bearing the wounds of love

    at those hands hovering over you to bless you.

What do you want to say to Jesus?

Watch carefully. He is leaving you now, being lifted out of sight. Soon he will be hidden by the cloud of God's presence.

Is there anything you want to do?

Anything you want to say?

Look at the two men dressed in white.

How does it feel to be in their presence?

Drink in their message:

    this same Jesus will come back.

'Jesus is coming back.'

Say that over and over to yourself.

How do you want to respond?

Stay silently on the mountain top for a few minutes.

Allow God to speak to you.

Be caught up in the wonder of the moment.

The others are going back to Jerusalem now.

Go with them.

Is anyone saying anything?

How do they seem to feel?

How do you feel?

See the city come into sight again.

Notice the dome of the Temple.

Hear the sounds

  see the sights   }   of the city.

    smell the smells

Go into the Temple with the others.

Try to drink in what you have seen and heard.

Thank God for it.

Whenever I embarked upon this type of meditation, it made a profound effect on my life. My meditation resulted in a genuine encounter with the living Christ. The result was a deep, inner communion with the Lord I love. Instead of just reading the Bible or expending effort on studying it, both valuable in themselves, its message was becoming internalised and personalised and therefore grew ever more precious. And my view of Jesus and my relationship with him was changing. On the one hand we were becoming more intimate, on the other more distant. I use the word 'distant' deliberately, not to suggest that Jesus was moving further away but to show that intimacy was laced with reverence and stripped of all hint of over-familiarity. I found I could not encounter Jesus in this genuine way and be 'matey'. That cheapened this 'tremendous lover'.

With the heart in the head

Campbell McAlpine says of meditation: 'Meditation is the devotional practice of pondering the words of a verse or verses of scripture, with a receptive heart, allowing the Holy Spirit to take the written Word and apply it as the living Word to the inner being... Someone has described meditation as "the digestive faculty of the soul..." Meditation is inwardly receiving the Word of God, illustrated by eating or feeding. God spoke to Ezekiel and emphasised this truth: "But you, son of man, *listen to* what I say... open your mouth and *eat* what I give you" (Ezek. 2:8, italics mine).[5]

For me, meditation was proving a most nourishing method of feeding on the Word of God.

It was much later that I discovered the value of *lectio divina*, or 'divine reading' as it is sometimes called. I had seen these two latin words on the timetable of the monastic day and had dismissed them thinking they had nothing to do with me, a layman. How wrong I was! *Lectio divina* is sometimes described as 'reading with the mind in the heart'. Basil Pennington strives to capture its value:

> [it is] reading with God, with the Holy Spirit – walking with Jesus on the way and letting his Spirit within us set our hearts ablaze as the scriptures are opened to us. This little method ... is more than reading: it is prayer, a real communication with God that opens out to us the depths and the heights – the depths of intimacy, the heights of transcendent contemplation ... It is not a question of reading a paragraph, a page, or a chapter. It is, rather, sitting down with a friend, the Lord, and letting him speak to us. We listen. And if what he says in the first word or the first sentence strikes us, we stop and let it sink in. We relish it. We respond from our heart. We enjoy it to the full before we move on. There is no hurry. We are sitting with our friend ... We let him speak. We really listen. [6]

I used this method of Bible reading more and more, interspersing it with the Ignatian approach and super-slow reading. Because, for me, ideas flow most fluently when I hold a pen in my hand, I would respond to the Lord and the passage before me in writing, recording my thoughts in my prayer journal. On one occasion, as I was reading the Song of Solomon meditatively, conscious because of certain sins that were cluttering my life, that I was unworthy of God's love, the familiar verse, 'He brought me to his banqueting table' begged me to stop. Among other things, this is how I responded to each word in turn:

HE:　Lord, it is you, the Lord of Lords and King of Kings, who have prepared that banqueting table. Such knowledge is too wonderful for me to take in. HE brought me. The high and lofty one, the Creator of the universe. I can call you my Beloved. You are mine. This is sheer, undeserved love. Last night I bewailed my own wretchedness and unworthiness to approach you, yet here this morning I hear your persistent, gentle, loving invitation. No. It is more than an invitation. You know that if you merely invited me at the moment, probably I would refuse to come. At least, I would be shy and hesitate. And so because you really want me to be there you

BROUGHT: me. What persistence! What desire! You love me enough to carry me, albeit struggling, to your banquet: the feast you have specially prepared. And if you are doing the carrying, all I have to do is to rest and relax and allow you to do what you will. With that, I am content and humbly thank you...

ME: I begin to see the banquet – carefully and lovingly laid out. I smell the fruit, see their colours, handle them, savour them in anticipation. And I see that it has been lovingly prepared. Amidst all this grandeur, as *your* specially invited guest, I see myself, and my heart cries out, 'Why me? I shouldn't be here!'

I go on to record the joy of receiving the forgiveness and cleansing and renewal with which God feasted me at his banqueting table on that occasion.

Richard Foster says of *lectio divina*: 'It is a kind of meditative spiritual reading in which the mind and the heart are drawn into the love and goodness of God ... We are doing more than reading words ... we are pondering all things in our heart as Mary did. We are entering into the reality of which the words speak.'[7]

As this happened in my experience more and more, the Bible assumed even greater importance in my listening to God. It was not just the framework into which all the other listening was required to fit. It was, of itself, the chief piece of listening equipment at my disposal. As such, it was always at my fingertips; whether studying it or memorising it or singing it or meditating on it, I would seek to open myself to God through its pages. Even so the problems did not disappear. On the contrary, they seemed to multiply, so much so that at times, for reasons I shall explain in the next chapter, I was tempted to give up.

Chapter 15

Tempted to Give Up

Ladislas Orsy makes the claim that, just as a skilled surgeon will operate on a patient better and faster than a medical student who has to keep referring to his text books, so an habitually prayerful person will discern God's still, small voice more quickly and more accurately than one whose prayer is spasmodic and dissipated.

This challenged me. I thought back to the early years of learning to listen, the honeymoon months when listening seemed pure delight. Then, the dire warnings I read and heard, 'listening to God is the most difficult yet most decisive part of prayer,'[1] and 'listening to God requires effort, practice and discipline,'[2] had puzzled me. Now the pressure was on me. The temptation to give up was one which plagued me often.

The pressing problem was busyness. Until 1981 I believed God was calling me to a life of listening prayer. This was to be the life-giving stream which never ceased to flow under the surface even while I managed my home and worked alongside my husband in the parish. I had carved out a place for God: in my home, in my heart and in my timetable. I determined, each day, to give him my undivided attention, quality time. And in the rhythm of the life which was mine at that time, I tried to lay the foundations of listening to God faithfully, through study and through prayer.

But in 1981, my first book was published. It was not that
I believed myself to be an author by vocation. I wrote this
one book because I was invited to do so. As far as I was
concerned, it was a one off. But this book on Christian
marriage spawned another book on engagement. Its
publication coincided with a prophecy I was given which
hinted that, since I would have no more children (I had
just had a hysterectomy) I was to give birth to books!

To my surprise, what I wrote seemed to strike a chord in
people's hearts. I was invited to speak at various meetings.
The number of couples queueing for counselling
increased. Suddenly, it seemed, I was catapulted from the
obscurity I relished into the whirlwind of activity I had so
often despised in others. Dispossessed of time, my
carefully planned routine lay in ruins. Concentrated
listening seemed a thing of the past.

A whole hour for prayer became a luxury, a fond
memory. Indeed, when ideas for a book or magazine article
flowed, prayer would often be squeezed out altogether.
Even if I lit my candle and contemplated the cross of Christ
in my prayer room, stillness evaded me. Quietness and
privacy simply swung open the door to a flood of
creativity: ideas for the next chapter of the book or for the
next talk I was to give would spring up like the magic
genies in children's stories.

Inwardly, I despaired. How was I to listen to God if I
had lost the art of stillness? At times I felt cheated. It was as
though my pearl of great price had been stolen almost
overnight. At other times guilt crushed me. What kind of a
Christian was I? God had given me such a valuable
training in prayer and here was I allowing it to be eclipsed
by activity.

In August 1982, I poured out some of the pain,
frustration and anguish in a letter to my friend and editor,
Derek Wood. I began the letter by complaining of a 'holy
restlessness, a yearning, an urgency to return to stillness -
not in an escapist way but to redress a balance.'! 'I'm in

conflict, inner turmoil. I know God has called me to a work of prayer. I know that power and authority and inspiration come in the stillness ... And yet I now take less time to be still. Whenever I'm involved in a project, I find stillness crowded out by thoughts and ideas which jostle and vie for attention.' Yet I wanted to be creative also: 'I have to be creative – God has shown me that. But that creativity has to arise from the silence ... What *is* the answer? How do I combine these seemingly incompatible responsibilities: to listen to God in the stillness *and* become a careful steward of the gifts he has entrusted me with?'

A few weeks before I wrote that letter I wrote in similar vein to another friend of mine, a hermit who is also a writer. As a fellow-traveller on the path of prayer, and as one who is far more experienced than I am, I awaited her advice with eagerness. Faithful friend that she is, she did not tell me what I wanted to hear: hang on to the luxury of your prolonged times of quiet; cling to this as your right. No. Instead, she explained that she believed that God was moving me on, that the luxury of the prolonged periods of prayer I had enjoyed in the past had served their purpose. By them God had brought me through my apprenticeship and at the same time had poured a great deal of healing into my life. Now, listening prayer was to serve a different purpose, among other things it was to fuel the fire of creativity rather than become an end in itself. In practical terms this meant that when I attempted to be still before God and ideas seemed to crowd God out, I must write the ideas down, see them as a part of the prayer, not enemies of it, recognise their source – God himself – and give him thanks.

The letter went on to warn that the intense activity in which I was now engaged must be punctuated by periods of uncluttered silence during which I could creep back into God for sustenance. This was essential for the survival of my life of listening. We have to be big for God.

As prayerful people, God wants us to grow even bigger for him. But we need to be very little too, so little that we know the joy of being carried and held by him.

These insights coincided with my editor's reaction to my letter:

> Your hermit friend wrote wisely I think. We do move from one of God's emphases for us to another. I am in need of learning more how to be silent. You have done that and need to learn how to use it, not as an end in itself, but as a means to a deeper friendship with God and a means of releasing your creativity. On the 'friendship with God' approach I can't help recalling what our church warden said about prayer. 'It's what God and I come up with together.' This describes creativity well, I think.

These letters had a certain ring of truth about them. Nevertheless, for several months I feared that I would never be capable of holding in tension the two vocations which were so dear to my heart: to be rooted in God and to be creative for him.

As I look back, with the wisdom of hindsight, I recognise that God was teaching me a vital lesson. I am a pilgrim. Pilgrims must be always on the move. A pilgrimage is a journey, often a steep ascent. I must face the challenge of the climb with a willingness to respond to the beckoning of God's finger no matter what it costs me. When he calls me to leave behind past securities and to face new challenges, I must obey, gladly and with child-like trust. Inherent in the Christian's calling is the belief that new life comes through death; the grain of wheat has to die so that it can produce new life. For the Christian, constant change is an inevitability.

But I had not learned these vital lessons at this stage of the journey and so I mourned for the loss of the pattern of prayer I had learned to value. And when God asked me to dismantle my prayer room and to pray, instead, in one corner of my study, this seemed yet another bitter blow, the loss of something else I had held dear.

Again, looking back, I understand what I did not appreciate at the time: God was asking me to piece together my work and my prayer. To move my cross and my candle and my prayer stool into my study simply symbolised this essential integration. But, at the time, I was full of pain. Clearly I had not yet learned another vital lesson the person of prayer must learn: to hold lightly to things and people and the past!

The underlying pain in me was not really touched until I read a book by Henri Nouwen in which he describes how his pursuit of prayer similarly had been disrupted by lecturing, writing, teaching. His honesty disarmed me:

> While teaching, lecturing, and writing about the importance of solitude, inner freedom, and peace of mind, I kept stumbling over my own compulsions and illusions... What was turning my vocation to be a witness to God's love into a tiring job? ... Maybe I spoke more about God than with him. Maybe my writing about prayer kept me from a prayerful life. Maybe I was more concerned about the praise of men and women than the love of God.[3]

Henri Nouwen plucked up the courage to clear his desk and his diary and become a Trappist monk for seven months. There, in the monastery, he reassessed his priorities with the help of the abbot. As his seven months of solitude drew to a close, he asked the abbot, John Eudes, how he was to combine prayer and creativity when he returned to the maelstrom of the college where he taught. John Eudes' advice to Nouwen reinforced the routine God had been suggesting to me through my friends:

* Establish a new rhythm of prayer, make it known,

and make it a priority.

* Make a daily discipline of listening prayer a must by plotting periods of the day when you determine that you will 'waste time' with God.

* Recurring days of retreat will be really fruitful only when this daily discipline is firmly established.

* Integrate prayer and work: 'Lecturing, preaching, writing, studying and counselling... would be nurtured and deepened by a regular prayer life.'[4]

As I pieced the jig-saw together, the picture which began to emerge pleased me. It presented me with the possibility of increased harmony in my life as I learned to blend personal preparation, time with people and prayer. I record in my prayer journal the joy that coursed through me as I re-apprenticed myself to the practice of listening prayer.

That is not to say I overcame the obstacles easily. I did not. Indeed, I still struggle to orchestrate prayer and work. But there were valuable lessons to be learned on the way.

The chief lesson God repeats to me over and over again is that if I am to receive his message into myself so that it strikes root, germinates and bears fruit, I need silence. This silence – 'Be still, and know that I am God' (Ps. 46:10) – is difficult to achieve. But it is the prerequisite of listening, and it involves telling myself, firmly and authoritatively, to stop chattering, to shut up!

Discipline is the answer. I find, for example, that when I resist the temptation to go straight from breakfast to my desk and start writing but, instead, move to my desk via my prayer corner, the quality of my work improves because, deliberately, I take time to drop anchor into God. I know this to be true. I have proved it over and over again.

Lack of obedience

But busyness was not the only hindrance to listening to God. Difficulties had pressed in on me before I started to write, problems of a more subtle nature. The chief problem was sin.

As I re-read my prayer journals today, the cacophony of anger, jealousy, resentment, poisoned memories and blatant disobedience which I describe in detail fills me with horror. There was the occasion when I poured out page after page of anger against a certain member of our congregation. Suddenly, it seemed, I stopped and wrote: 'Lord, I've just heard the birds singing. My anger has been shouting so loudly, I haven't heard them until now.' I had been sitting in the garden for a whole hour!

But it was the disobedience which seriously threatened my relationship with God. With shame, I now read my own accounts of my struggle to give God the mastery in certain relationships which were corroding my friendship with Jesus. I wanted the best of both worlds: my way and God's.

When God faced me with the inevitable choice – my way *or* his – I squealed. For months I was so full of self-will that I heard little from the still, small voice of God. Bible meditation ceased, Bible study stopped. I would dip into the Bible from time to time but it communicated nothing. This was hardly surprising. I had not yet learned that God's Word is not simply to be studied, read or personalised. It has to be obeyed. But as William Barclay warns: 'There are people into whose minds [and emotions] the word has no more chance of gaining an entry than the seed has of settling into the ground that has been beaten hard by many feet.'[5]

There are many things which can close a person's mind. Disobedience is the most effective. As someone aptly said: 'The one who truly listens is also the one who truly obeys.'

It hurts to recall the failures. It is the kind of hurt I felt once when I watched a family on the beach in Cyprus. The

parents were trying hard to give their children a happy
holiday. The sun was shining, the sandy beach stretched
for miles, white waves tickled the shore. And the children
were squabbling over a small, red, plastic spade.

I am like those children. God's generosity to me had
known no limits. Yet I was throwing his love back in his
face because the attractions the world offered seemed to
possess a greater magnetic power than the wonder of his
presence. At times I rejected him altogether. At times I
feared my life of listening was a closed chapter.

But the Holy Spirit continued to bombard my ears with
messages from God: uncomfortable messages, disconcerting messages, messages which troubled me and caused
me to struggle to survive. I would hear these messages and
take careful note of them. And I would respond to them in
my prayer journal, not recognising that the Spirit's work
is not always to notify us of God's love but rather to bring
us up with a jolt: to show us his displeasure.

Little by little, my response grew stronger. Eventually,
God showed me what had to be done. A load of rubble had
to be tipped out on the dumping ground of the cross where
he would take responsibility for it. Slowly and thought-
fully I made a reappraisal of my life: where I was going,
what I was wanting, what God was asking of me.
Anything which obstructed the path would have to go.
Equally slowly, but quite deliberately, I cleared out the
clutter which had kept me from Christ.

I see now what was happening. God emptied me of so
much of self that he created within me a greater capacity
for him. He had read the signs which showed that, at the
deepest level of my being, this was what I wanted. When
my Bible lay unused, a hunger would grow inside me.
When my prayer time became nothing more than good
and evil waging war within, a holy dissatisfaction filled
me. It gave birth to the realisation that I cannot live
without him, that a life devoid of listening to him, loving
him and being met by him spells emptiness and not

fullness. The good would therefore have to win.

I would like to be able to present a neat formula which I used to steer me through these sticky patches. Alas! I know of no such aerobics guaranteed to keep me spiritually trim and fit to listen. The struggles I have described still dog my path of prayer from time to time just as they have done in the past.

Obedience, I know, is the key, the 'open sesame' to listening. For years God engraved that word on my heart. For this reason I have studied the salutary warnings the Bible gives to the disobedient. I have combed the pages of the Bible in an attempt to discover what God requires of me in certain situations: as a wife, a mother, a friend, a business woman; as a sexual being, a female and one entrusted with Christian leadership. I know that disobedience can lock and bolt the door against God's still, small voice. Even so, I find it easier to write about obedience, read about obedience and preach about obedience than to obey. I know how to leap this hurdle: simply discover God's will and do it. But I find it hard.

The same stubbornness characterises my current attitude to stillness. I love it. I benefit from it. Yet I neglect it because I persuade myself that the pressures on me do not allow it space. I know the way out of the problem: respond to the wooing of God. Yet I ignore his courtship.

But God's patience seems infinite. When I do succumb to my self-imposed discipline, I recognise that the long apprenticeship was not wasted. I drop into stillness easily and quickly. The awareness of God's life springs into being equally rapidly. That is hardly surprising since God is never reluctant to come to our aid but responds gladly to every advance of ours. The joy of surrendering to him is usually sweet. A privilege. And being found, held, and loved by God all over again and receiving his activity deep into the inner recesses of my being fills me with fresh awe and wonder and praise. The encounter is usually so powerful that it leaves me asking the question: '*Why* don't

I make more time for this more often?'

Because such encounters with God seemed fleeting and few and far between I discovered that my hermit friend was correct when she recommended uncluttered times with God away from the normal, hectic routine. I am now busier than I was when I first faced the crisis I described at the beginning of this chapter. For this reason I try to spend a day away each month when God and I can 'just be' together in the quietness of a prayer saturated place. I aim to arrive at 9.30a.m. and not to leave before 7.0p.m. During these quiet days of reflective, listening prayer, time seems to stand still. Nine hours seem like twenty-four. On some of these days apart, I asked God to show me how to be more effective in integrating my work and my prayer. It was on one such occasion that the phrase 'praying my life' captured my imagination and encouraged me further to perfect the art of finding God in everything.

Chapter 16
Some Helps along the Way

Martha, the one distracted by a thousand tasks, and Mary, the one who lost herself in the wonder of Christ's company, can co-exist in the same person. And this need not result in spiritual schizophrenia. Certain practical methods of prayer make this unlikely marriage possible.

When this realisation burst in to my awareness, I began to ask God to help me to tune into him, not only in times of stillness, but at odd times during the day. In order to thus pray my life more effectively, I used one retreat to explore how others did this. From there I went on to experiment for myself.

The first suggestion which fascinated me was what Guy Brinkworth calls 'the method of the godly pause'.[1] In his book, *Thirsting for God*, he explains how this occasional pause during the day to say the name of Jesus or simply reflect on the fact that he is concerned for us can be a valuable 'booster' to the prayer of listening.

This seemed so sensible, almost obvious, that I adopted this practice immediately. When taking paper out of my typewriter or making myself a cup of coffee or waiting at traffic lights, I would turn my mind God-wards quite deliberately. Often God would communicate his presence to me in some felt way.

And a phrase of Catherine de Hueck Doherty captured my imagination also. She speaks of the 'little pools of silence' which punctuate one's day and goes on to demonstrate how prayer might feature in these so that the desert experiences of our life might be irrigated constantly. Whilst washing up, ironing, hoovering, dusting, gardening, walking to the post, driving to the shops, or travelling by public transport, therefore, I would try to listen to God as intently as in my place of prayer. It worked.

Soon after my resolve to tune into God all day and every day, I was caught in a sudden, heavy snowstorm which caused traffic chaos almost immediately. It took me four hours to drive along a route which normally takes half an hour: an excellent way to put into practice my intention. That day I learned the truth of Catherine of Siena's claim: 'Every time and every place is a time and place for prayer.' I also understood why it was said of St Teresa of Avila that she could find God 'so easily among the pots and pans' and why Brother Lawrence testified that even when, as cook of the monastery, he was elbow-deep in potato peelings, he could converse with God, entreat him, rejoice with a thousand thanksgivings; how his very soul, without any forethought, could be lifted above all earthly things and be held by God.

Even bedtime became a time of resting in God as I tried to follow the psalmist's example:

On my bed I remember you;
I think of you through the watches of the night (Ps. 63:6).

The more I pursued this path of prayer, the more I would wake in the night, not from insomnia but with a burden to pray: for a particular person, for nurses on duty, for people who become suicidal in the loneliness of the long night hours. One night I woke with the name of a member of our congregation ringing in my mind: a pregnant wife. I prayed. I was moved the next day when her husband telephoned to say that his wife had given birth to a daughter in the middle of that night.

And in my waking hours, I delighted to discover the reality of another of Guy Brinkworth's prayer boosters: the recollection of the constant companionship of Christ: 'As I work, a Loved Presence over my shoulder, as I drive a Loved Passenger beside me. In my reading, cooking, studying, whilst teaching, nursing, accounting: in the maelstrom of the supermarket or waiting for the bus or train – ever the loving sense of a Presence – always that nostalgia for my Creator.'[2]

Gradually I learned to phase in and out of a loving awareness of Christ and his presence on and off during the day. I found that the warmth of the encounter with Christ in the early morning stillness need not vanish as I apply myself to work. Rather, the experience was not unlike the love which holds two friends together. They may not meet, but they will think about one another during the day, wonder how the other is faring, picture the other, even make a mental note of snippets of news to be shared when they next telephone or see one another. Thus the friendship is kept alive in the absences; the communication between them never really ceases.

Short ejaculatory prayers can help to keep this love alive. A prayer of Amy Carmichael's was one I used often: 'Holy Spirit, think through me till your ideas become my ideas.' And John Wesley's words expressed my desire to stay in tune all day: 'Jesus, strengthen my desire to work and speak and think for you.' Especially while writing or counselling. Samuel's short prayer frequently found an echo on my lips: 'Speak, Lord, your servant is listening.'

Using simple, practical techniques like this, I discovered that listening prayer need not be divorced from my everyday routine, but could become an integral part of it. As Guy Brinkworth puts it: 'a background yearning for God can be sustained in the middle of any activity as a kind of "celestial music while you work".'[3] 'The internal burning sign of love need not, with practice and adaptation, interfere with the efficiency of the "secular" side of the contemplative's activity.'[4] In-tuneness with God's will and mind need not cease when we take up a pen or a newspaper or a gardening fork.

I am not saying I became a Martha, so harassed by frenetic activity that I could see God only out of the corner of one eye; I am saying that I began to experiment with allowing the Mary who is a part of me to sit at the feet of Jesus in leisurely, listening and adoring prayer at the beginning of the day, but to give the Martha, who is also a part of the real me, permission to live life to the full without losing the sense of Jesus's attentive presence. Sometimes this seemed easy. At other times, almost impossible.

Spiritual reading

Spiritual reading featured largely in the life of the people of prayer whose pilgrimage was influencing my own, as indeed, I discovered, it had done in the lives of the great teachers of prayer of the past. St Teresa of Avila, the Carmelite mystic, often went to prayer with a book in her hand. She once wrote: 'Often the mere fact that I had it by me was enough. Sometimes I read a little, sometimes a great deal.'[5]

Spiritual reading usually takes one of four forms:

* instruction: when we read about prayer in parti-
        cular or the spiritual life in general

* inspiration: when what we read encourages us to
        grow in the life of listening to God and our entire
        relationship with him

* preparation: reading matter which prepares us to
        tune in to God

* meditation: when our reading acts as a prayer
        guide.

I learned so much from the sayings of the Early Fathers and from the classics on prayer: Thomas Merton, Pierre de Caussade, Thomas à Kempis, Carlo Carretto, to name but a few, that the temptation was to substitute reading about prayer for the discipline itself of listening to God. But I was particularly grateful for the instruction and inspiration spiritual reading gave me. I remember reading St Bernard's reflections on the difficulty which dogged me – of combining action and contemplation – and the relief with which I reacted to *his* suggestion that, since Martha and Mary are sisters, they should live together harmoniously under the same roof. They should seek to complement one another.

And I recall the hope that surged through me as a powerful picture from *Poustinia* whetted my appetite for more effective listening to God:

> The world is cold. Someone must be on fire so that people can love and put their cold hands and feet against that fire. If anyone allows this to happen . . . then he will become a fireplace at which men can warm themselves. His rays will go out to the ends of the earth.

> The English word 'zeal' usually means intensity of action. But real zeal is standing still and letting God be a bonfire in you. It's not very easy to have God's fire within you. Only if you are possessed of true zeal will you be able to contain God's bonfire. We must allow God to 'contribute' through us . . . [6]

Or again: 'The Lord is calling us to *stand still before him while walking with men.* Yes, the next step . . . is the ability to walk with men and be contemplatives while we are walking.' [7]

A Prayer Journal
Michel Quoist's *Prayers of Life* were a constant source of

inspiration. In them, the author, a Roman Catholic priest, points out his true feelings to God, then records God's response:

> I'm at the end of my tether, Lord.
> I am shattered,
> I am broken.
> Since this morning I have been struggling to escape temptation, which, now subtle, now persuasive, now tender, now sensuous, dances before me like a glamour girl at a fair.
> I don't know what to do.
> I don't know where to go.
> It spies on me, follows me, engulfs me.
> When I leave a room I find it seated and waiting for me in the next ...
> Lord, Lord, help me!
>
> Son, I am here.
> I haven't left you.
> How weak is your faith!
>
> You are too proud.
> You still rely on yourself.
> If you want to surmount all temptations, without falling or weakening, calm and serene,
> You must surrender yourself to me ...
> You must let yourself be guided like a child,
> My little child.[8]

This method of communication with God attracted me. When, in the course of my spiritual reading, I bumped into the suggestion that the beginner in listening prayer should attempt at least some writing, I needed no further invitation. As I have explained, I found that, for me, writing was a powerful method of concentrating. With a pen in my hand and a note-book on my knee, I would write my daily letter to God, telling him how life was treating me. In this way, my own thoughts and emotions would clarify. I would then pause, listen, maybe meditate on a Bible passage or an object, and go on to write down anything I believed God was saying or showing me in response. As I look back now on nine years of such journal keeping, I marvel at the way God used this method of communication both to deepen my relationship with him and to point out some uncomfortable home truths about myself.

Once, when I complained that there was so little time to pray on Sundays, God seemed to say: 'What about church services?' I laughed. As a vicar's wife, going to church came into the 'work' category. I think of Sunday as a working day. My husband and I have our 'Sabbath' in the week. At church there are people to see, people's needs to minister to, responsibilities to shoulder. But God turned this attitude inside out so that I began to go to services expectant: waiting for God to say at least one thing which was pertinent to my walk with him at that moment, listening, too, to the wonder of who he is as expressed by the composers of some of our magnificent hymns, and of course, listening to his Word, the Bible.

And more and more God 'spoke' through music. In church, if I was battered emotionally for any reason, music would be the ointment the Holy Spirit applied to the inner wounds. If I came to my place of prayer fraught by the pressures of the day, music would woo me into the stillness where God's presence is most powerfully felt. Through meditative music, God would seem to speak: of his longing to invade my spirit with the Spirit, of his consoling love, of his agony on the cross, of his gift of forgiveness. Some music would cause a stirring in my heart and set a fountain of praise playing inside me. It was as though the many layers of my personality responded to God in different ways. Music filtered through to touch and communicate with the secret, hidden parts which rarely respond to words.[9]

But the word which percolated from God through each of these methods of listening was 'obedience'. It was as though he was underlining constantly the fact that listening to him must result in obeying him. God's lament over the disobedient filled me with pain:

> If only you had paid attention to my commands,
>   your peace would have been like a river,
>   your righteousness like the waves of the sea. (Isa. 48:18).

And Jesus's stern observation reinforced the realisation that obedience is a prerequisite for rootedness in God:

> Therefore everyone who hears these words of mine and puts them into practice is like a wise man who built his house on the rock. The rain came down, the streams rose, and the winds blew and beat against that house; yet it did not fall, because it had its foundation on the rock (Matt. 7:24–25).

Such obedience to the Father, I knew, characterised the life of Jesus. Such obedience was the source of the psalmist's joy (Ps. 119:111). Such obedience brought happiness to the author of Proverbs (Prov. 8:34). The implication was clear: if I wanted to enjoy unruffled peace and if I wanted to keep the lines of communication open between God and me, I, too, must progress in the life of obedience. As Kenneth Leach rightly reminds us, 'There can be no spiritual life if ethical demands are bypassed or sins ignored.'[10]

I was grateful that, from time to time, God brought across my path people of prayer who could help me in this superhuman task. I would have floundered abysmally without their spiritual direction.

Contemplative prayer and listening to God are dis-

ciplines which lay the Christian wide open to eccentricities, extremes and errors. To protect them from sallying
forth on some mystical ego-trip most people find that a
mentor and guide to set them on course from time to time
is essential. Thus St. Basil (330–379) urges his readers to
find a man 'who may serve you as a very sure guide in the
work of leading a holy life', one who knows 'the straight
road to God'. He warns that 'to believe that one does not
need counsel is great pride.'[11] St Jerome (340–420) pleads
with his friend Rusticus not to set out on an uncharted
way without a guide. And St Augustine (354–430) is
emphatic: 'No one can walk without a guide.'[12]

Not everyone would agree that spiritual direction
should be given by a friend. Nevertheless, I was grateful for
the friendship I enjoyed with those to whom I turned for
help along the way. To me, they were 'soul friends', to
borrow Kenneth Leach's memorable phrase.

A soul friend is the intimate stranger who, as a person
experienced in the life of prayer, will commit himself to
you in an adult/adult relationship in an attempt to set you
on the path of prayer, assist you in discerning the
breathings of the Spirit, bring you to a place of greater self-
knowledge and self-acceptance and help you find the will
of God. The soul friend will avoid encouraging excessive
dependence on himself, but will accept you as you are as
well as confront and challenge when occasion demands. A
soul friend might draw alongside the person of prayer as
he confesses his failures to God. Or he might be God's
instrument of healing using prayer counselling, the
laying-on of hands or anointing with oil. To those of us
who have been privileged to receive the help of a soul
friend, a certain Celtic saying elicits a loud 'Amen':
'Anyone without a soul friend is a body without a head.'[13]

It was my soul friend, a spiritual guide, who listened to
my confusion on more than one occasion. With him the
jumble of conflicting thoughts and emotions would
tumble out. With him I could express my uncertainties

and fears. He would listen, attune his ear to the Holy Spirit of God, disentangle the threads, present them with order and clarity and explore with me what God was asking of me. He would make suggestions but never demand that I obey him implicitly.

I remember clearly one of those horrifying patches when God seemed to have absented himself never to return, when I recorded in my prayer journal that a complete revulsion for prayer swamped me. Engulfed by this darkness, and in panic, I telephoned this friend and asked if I could see him. Sensing the depths of my despair he fixed an appointment for the following day. As I described the darkness, the fear, the nothingness, the pain, I also voiced my self-doubts: Had I sinned? Was that why God had disappeared? Was I deluding myself about this pilgrimage of prayer? Was I expecting too much, expecting to encounter God in the way I had enjoyed? Or were the doors to contemplation and listening to God closing?

When my tale of woe had been told, this wise man of God closed his eyes, held his head in his hands, and went quite silent. I knew him well enough to know that he would be praying. A hush stole over the room and I waited.

After several minutes he looked up and I noticed that his eyes twinkled and an excited smile spread across his face. 'Joyce!' he said, 'I feel so excited by this darkness of yours. You see, when you stand in the howling desert like this, you never know how God will next come to you. What you do know is that he will come. I believe God is encouraging you to look for him round every corner because he *is* coming – and he's coming soon.'

This calm, sensitive, positive challenge, this absence of blame or finger-pointing criticism, this freedom to talk in this way to someone who understood the inner turmoil because he was an experienced navigator on the voyage of prayer was precisely what I needed. That day we knelt together in silence in his prayer room. The presence of a fellow-voyager symbolised, for me, the objective fact that God had not left me. When my friend left, I lingered. As I gazed at the crucifix hanging on his hessian-covered wall, with its reminder that Jesus, himself, had known the darkness of separation from the Father, courage flowed right into my grazed and troubled spirit. Later, having absorbed the stillness and basked in it, the heaviness lifted; my steps were lighter as I walked away.

It was this friend who taught me how to reap the harvest of meditation and share the fruit with others. It was he who instilled in me the courage to face myself as I really am: not the successful, coping person I like to project to the world, but the mixture of success and failure, honesty and deception, saint and sinner which I really am. It was he who confronted me with the need to change. His own pilgrimage of prayer proved to me that listening to God is a journey whose joys are found as much in the travelling as in the arriving. His child-likeness in prayer drew from me a child-like eagerness to reach my destination even when the destination, I knew, lay at least in part on the other side of eternity.

These aids to listening spurred me on. I was always hungry for more. Someone has described this urgency well:

Saint Catherine of Siena, Lord,
said you are like the sea.
The more we know of you,
  the more we find;
And the more we find of you,
the more we want.
Yet we never really understand you.

I don't like that idea at all.
I want to know about you, Lord.
Just as I want to know about the sea
or space or electricity.

But if it's true that I can't know it all
Then keep me wanting to know.[14]

Chapter 17

More Helps along the Way

To listen to God I need silence: internal silence and external silence. But our world is polluted by noise which, like a persistent drum-roll, drowns God's voice, or at least distorts it.

Screwtape, the senior devil in C. S. Lewis' book, *The Screwtape Letters,* divulges one of the reasons for this perpetual cacophony:

> Music and silence – how I detest them both!... no square inch of infernal space and no moment of infernal time has been surrendered to either of those abominable forces, but all has been occupied by Noise – Noise, the grand dynamism, the audible expression of all that is exultant, ruthless and virile... We will make the whole universe a noise in the end. We have already made great strides in this direction as regards the Earth. The melodies and silences of Heaven will be shouted down in the end.[1]

There were times when the external noises in my own home banished the still, small voice of God. Ordinary, domestic noises – the sound of the radio, the shriek of the telephone, the songs my husband sings in the mornings – could prevent me from putting up the shutters of the senses to drop deep into the silence of God. For this reason, the regular Quiet Day and an occasional retreat quickly became priorities as I have said. I learned to plot these in my diary first and to fit other engagements round them because these times when God and I could 'just be' together became vital times of renewal, refreshment and reappraisal.

The Anglican convent near my home is a hiding place where I delight to spend a day in quietness. A large converted manor house, it stands in spacious grounds and overlooks acres of farmland. When I go there for a day, I accept this solitude as a gift of God's grace. To me the time and place are sacred.

The first points around which I plan the day are the Communion service and lunch. Within that framework I create space for a leisurely time of listening prayer which will not be short-circuited by a gong or a bell or the need to depart. Apart from these three focal points, I expect to benefit from a period of spiritual reading, meditation and writing in my prayer journal. Work is refused permission to come with me unless part of my listening is to ask God whether I should accept a particular invitation to speak, or to seek guidance about a piece of writing I am working on.

I try to begin the day by dropping consciously into the creativity of God's silence. The garden helps. I might stand under the ancient cedar tree and gaze at its strength, the circumference of its branches and the size of the cones. Or if the weather is warm I might sit beside the pond, contemplate its plump gold fish and mull over those words of one of the mystics: 'We are in God as a fish is in water.' Or I might wander among the daffodils or the bluebells or sit under the japonica. I refuse to hurry. Most of my week I rush from one meeting to the next or scamper from one appointment to the next. As my body adapts to walking instead of hurrying, my mind and emotions wind down also. At the same time the level of expectancy rises as I realise that I am in this place for one purpose only: to hear God speak. I try to be open to him at every stage of the day and in every corner of the convent. Sometimes he creeps up on me when I least expect it: as I absorb the beauty of his creation in the garden, while I muse on the sufferings of Christ depicted in the stations of the cross in the chapel, while a sister reads as we eat in the refectory in silence. On these holy days God always seems to drop something into my quietened heart which I need to hear. That is why it seems sensible, not selfish, to organise my activities around this stillness. Through it, I catch my spiritual breath, rest in him afresh, and gain his perspective.

This is the purpose of a Quiet Day. One of the desert fathers expressed it simply but powerfully. Into a jar he poured water and some sand. As he shook the jar, the water became murky, but as he allowed the jar to rest the sand settled to the bottom and the water became clear again. Using this visual aid, he taught his disciples that the pace people live their lives normally clouds their spiritual perspective. Those who dare to settle themselves into God's stillness find that the water of perception becomes clear again.

I value these sacred spaces more and more and know that my life and ministry are impoverished when I permit them to be elbowed out of my diary. The busier I am, the more I attempt to find God in everything, the more I need to stand in that still point with God where my looking becomes a beholding, my listening an attentive hearing, my touching a deep awareness, and my tasting a silent savouring. God's gift of a Quiet Day provides me with a sip of some of these spiritual liqueurs.

By admitting that this need to withdraw from the world's whirlpool is an urgent one, I am not saying that it is impossible to 'find God everywhere and in everything'. What I am saying is that in times of quiet it is easier to listen to God attentively. Listening to God, as we have seen already in this book, involves so much more than the narrow sphere of hearing a voice. It involves a tuning-in to a multi-level method of communication: hearing a voice, yes, but a presence also – and signs and non-verbal communication and everything which goes into creating a relationship.

It is rather like my relationship with my husband. He and I work hard at communicating with each other. We give one another quality time most days because in this way we believe we keep our marital love alive. Even so our holidays are a highlight: an indispensable part of the oneness we enjoy. On holiday we draw closer to one another than ever before because we have the leisure to listen to each other with every fibre of our beings.

Similarly I need to take time out to be with God. For me, a day seems too short to descend into the depths of the grand silence of God. A three or four day retreat gives far more scope for the letting go of anxieties and distractions and obsessions which is a precursor of in-depth listening to the awareness of God.

Again I am fortunate. Seven years ago a friend suggested that I should make a retreat at one of the houses of another Anglican community, the Sisters of the Love of God. This was more easily accessible to my home than Whitby and its size and intimacy appealed immediately: only five or six sisters live and pray together there. In Holy Week 1978 I spent three days there and it has been my spiritual home ever since. There I hide occasionally for three or four days and my prayer journal reminds me how rich and healing, how challenging and life-transforming these days have been.

The cross which hangs from the ceiling of this chapel is unique. On one side the artist has painted a picture of the crucified Christ. On the other he has painted a portrayal of the resurrected Lord. I love to kneel at the foot of that cross and savour the mysteries of our salvation. Usually, my concentration focuses on Christ's suffering and sacrifice. But one morning, after Communion, as I stayed in the chapel to pray, the Holy Spirit drew my attention to the living Lord. What I 'heard' in the silence was not new factually. It *was* new experientially. I revelled in the revelation, took my prayer journal to the bottom of the garden, sat on a log under the pine trees and tried to capture the wonder:

Lord, thank you. I feel as though I've taken one delicious bite, the first of many, from an exotic fruit. I *know* that you are alive. It's as though I've never heard that message before. It is exhilarating; wonderful... You are alive. You are life. You are my life...

Lord, I began to realise that for forty years, and particularly for the past four or so, I've contemplated Gethsemane and Calvary and Easter Saturday but I've never, in fact, identified with Easter Day. But that gap between Calvary and Pentecost leaves an inexplicable void. Thank you that you've filled in the gap – placed in my hands the missing piece of the jig-saw. It's exciting... Oh! How much joy has yet to be entered into.

Revelations like these broadened my view of God. Sometimes God spoke to me about the nitty-gritty of life, like my marriage. One day, I marvelled at the way God was bringing healing to our marriage:

Thank you, dearest Lord, for this retreat: for the weather, the hot days, the golden dawns and dusks. Thank you for time to reflect on our marriage. Thank you that for twenty years David has coped with all my immature comings and goings and with all my struggling and striving. Thank you that his has been the love that will not let me go and which is enabling the butterfly to emerge from the chrysalis. What a wonderful husband you provided me with. Thank you, dear Lord, for this provision for my deepest need. And thank you for this love of ours which goes so much deeper than superficialities and anchors us in one another and in you.

Sometimes God's word winged its way into my awareness with supernatural force. At a time when I was crawling out of the tunnel of depression but still dogged with a recurring death wish, I bumped into this quotation in one of Alexander Schmemann's books: 'I shall not die but LIVE and declare the works of the Lord.' I wept. I knew God wanted me to echo those words. In many ways, this was a turning point as I received from him the courage to make those words my own.

I do not always go to a convent to make my retreat. Sometimes I use a cottage in the country where I read and meditate and reflect and study God's word and pray. The advantage of a cottage retreat, for me, is that, surrounded by the wonders of God's creation, I open hidden parts of myself to God which remain closed elsewhere. I listen as I walk. God speaks through the silent eloquence of the countryside.

But to retreat in the context of a worshipping, praying community adds an indefinable ingredient to this time of attentiveness to God. And so I vary my venue.

If I stay in a convent, I drop into the rhythm of life observed by the sisters: I eat when they eat, worship when they worship, read when they read, and sometimes work in the garden alongside them. I sleep more than they do. I am not embarrassed to make this confession. I am usually in need of rest when I retreat. Sleep is a gift of God and the ability to listen increases when the body is rested.

These retreats are not necessarily sublime mountain-top experiences. Sometimes they prove painful, often challenging. On one retreat, I recorded my resolve:

*   to rid myself of the rubble of resentment: 'prayer and resentment cannot co-exist'

*   to re-instate Jesus on the throne of my life: I cannot listen accurately to him if he has a rival

    to try harder to respond to the challenge of inter-twining listening prayer and writing.

At times I record the specific instructions God seemed to be giving: at a time when the music group in our church was without a leader, God seemed to nudge me in that direction in a way that took me completely by surprise. I spent much of the retreat resisting God's challenge but eventually capitulated: 'Lord, if the music group is where you want me, I *am* willing. Make me more ready to accept the cost which I have counted.'

When I make a three or four day retreat, I bring to it four main aims:

*   to realise more clearly the presence of God in the inner sanctuary of my being

*   to assess the response I have been making to God's loving overtures since my last retreat

*   to discern what God's will is for me in the here and now

*   to readjust my life in the light that God gives.

In my prayer journal, I usually spell out my hopes and fears to God almost as soon as I arrive. Day by day I write to him and record his response. I often scribble quotations from my spiritual reading in this fat note-book. The fruit of my meditations is also captured there. At the end of the retreat, I keep a page called 'Retreat Resolves'. On this page, I write down God's re-commissioning for the coming months.

Several questions require examination and an honest answer during these times apart:

* Does anything in my life stand between God and me?

* Is anything preventing me from giving myself freely to fulfil God's plan for my life?

* What have I been doing for God?

* What am I doing for him at present?

* What ought I to be doing?

This ruthless self-examination usually results in a prolonged period of confession. Keeping short accounts with God in this way is essential. When sin curdles within, I am not in a position to hear God speaking. Isaiah reminds us of the solemn fact that sin separates us from God: 'Your iniquities have separated you from your God; your sins have hidden his face from you, so that he will not hear' (Isa. 59–2). Simon Tugwell, commenting on this gulf, warns the would-be listener that to fail to see this is sloppy. And Henri Nouwen observes that if the person of prayer persists in clutching sin in his clammy hands as though it were a priceless treasure, he is unable to receive from God in the here and now.

Slowly and gradually God convinced me of the uselessness of rummaging around in my own sin and of the value of confession. Confession precipitates the desire to change. It gives birth to repentance: the determination to live differently. It syringes the ear which would tune in to God.

Almost always I would confess my failings to God privately. But there came a time in my life when God persuaded me to take the Bible's advice seriously; to avail myself of the opportunity of confessing my sin in the presence of a shrewd and trusted friend (Jas. 5:16).

The depression with which God entrusted me pushed me into laying aside my pride and seeking help of this nature. While the cloud of depression hung over me, from time to time I would struggle with suicidal tendencies as the desire to live evaporated. At times I sunk so low that I considered it my right to think this way.

When a friend pointed out to me one day that this desire to cease to be was not so much a sickness as a sin, I was shocked. If this was true I had sinned seriously and persistently. When I tried to confess this deep-seated rebellion to God I became guilt-ridden, inwardly tortured, introspective. The realisation dawned, therefore, that I had nothing to lose and everything to gain by taking this sin to God in the presence of a prayerful friend. The same friend I mentioned in the last chapter agreed to pray with me as I repeated my confession to God.

Of course, I was not confessing *to* the spiritual guide. I was clear in my mind that it was God I was addressing. I used the form of confessional which is recognised in the Anglican Church: a short formal prayer which does not give scope for excusing oneself or blaming others but which encourages the penitent to take full responsibility for what he has done: 'I confess . . . I have sinned.'

When I heard myself name the sin 'suicide', it stripped me of all the pretence with which I had clothed myself for months. This was valuable in itself. But when I heard this spiritual guide pronounce the absolution from John's epistle: 'If we confess our sins, he is faithful and just and will forgive us our sins and purify us from all unrighteousness' (1 John 1:9), and I heard him proclaim in the name and on the authority of Jesus: 'You are totally forgiven . . . Christ has set you free,' it was as though the shackles of guilt and condemnation fell from me. I knew I was free to walk away from these chains which had bound me.

The confession made, we talked about the implications of what I had just done. First, this counsellor, friend and guide suggested that I should read a book entitled *The Cloud of Unknowing*. I had read this classic on prayer before. As I re-read it, I understood why he had recommended it as a follow-up to the ministry I had received. The book contains invaluable insights on sin and failure and persistence in approaching God.

The reading of this book was to be my 'penance'. The word startled me. True Protestant that I am, I had always reacted negatively to the word 'penance'. I thought it meant punishment. Indeed, the Pocket Oxford Dictionary defines the word in this way: 'punishment inflicted on oneself especially under priestly direction'. Now I saw that penance need not mean to rub the penitent's nose in his own filth, nor to force him to pay the penalty of his misconduct. Rather it can have positive connotations. Penance can make a constructive contribution to the spiritual growth of the Christian.

My own first taste of confession and penance is a good example. I could have come away from this experience feeling condemned by God and my confidante. Instead, my friend and I talked about the reason for my visit: the death wish. This spiritual guide made no attempt to excuse my sin. What he did do was to disentangle the sin from the need which had given birth to the sin: emotional wounds which would not stop bleeding. He explained that the sinful element had been dealt with through the confession and Christ's forgiveness; the emotional need would be met in a different way. By inviting me to read the book, *The Cloud of Unknowing*, he believed that some of my confusion would be clarified and I would glean insights which were essential to this stage of the pilgrimage of prayer. When I read the book, the mists of confusion did lift. I was delivered from the stranglehold of introspection and I rejoiced in this particular piece of penance.

Such positive penance given by an experienced and wise soul friend can be a constructive way of setting us on our feet again after we have fallen. It is one of the contributions a soul friend makes to our spiritual growth. As an objective observer he can discern more clearly than oneself where God wants to purge and prune and where he wants to bind up and heal. Kenneth Leach suggests other reasons why a soul friend is of value: he helps us to laugh at ourselves, relax, not to take ourselves too seriously, not to assume a false piety. I needed this spiritual guide to do this for me.

Fasting

Fasting, I found, was another sin-and-pain detector. I would embark on a thirty-six hour fast and expect to feel super-holy. Instead, by the time the fast had finished, I might have snapped at my children, been irritable with my husband or chewed over some resentment which I had been scarcely aware of earlier. Richard Foster explains why fasting highlights huge inconsistencies or seedling sins germinating in our life:

> Fasting reveals the things that control us... We cover up what is inside us with food and other good things, but in fasting these things surface. If pride controls us, it will be revealed almost immediately... Anger, bitterness, jealousy, strife, fear – if they are within us, they will surface during fasting. At first we will rationalise that our anger is due to our hunger, then we know that we are angry because the spirit of anger is within us.[2]

But fasting, I found, not only exposes the large lumps of wax in my spiritual ears, it makes a positive contribution to listening prayer. Perhaps its major contribution is the uncluttered, purposeful space it provides for the act of listening to God. When I fast, with no meals to prepare and no clearing up to do, I can linger in my prayer corner and listen to God without having to keep an eye on the clock.

In one sense, fasting of itself does not aid my ability to concentrate on God in that I am often acutely aware of my rumbling tummy or the headache which often plagues me at such times or the occasional dizziness which reminds me that I have not eaten for several hours. Yet, in another sense, the discipline of the fast, with its non-verbal commitment to hear God's presence or voice, makes a major contribution to listening prayer. The physical symptoms remind me of the purpose of this fast: prayer and attentive listening to God.

Catherine of Siena and Teresa of Avila, whose teachings on prayer have inspired Christians down the ages, believed that unless a Christian spends time tuning in to an awareness of God, then much of the energy spent in other things is a waste of time. As this belief lodged itself in me, more and more I experimented with these aids to prayer, adopting Archbishop William Laud's prayer: 'Lord, I am coming as fast as I can.'

Chapter 18

Another Piece of the Scaffolding: the Listening Group

'No man is an island,' claimed John Donne. No Christian attempting to pray is an island either. My individual listening, if it is to bear lasting fruit, must be healthily integrated into the Body of Christ. For this reason, I need others.

For years the independent part of me which enjoys going it alone rejected this need for others. But when God added to me a group of like-minded people, as intent on learning to hear the Spirit's breathings as I was, a whole new dimension of listening to God opened up for me. I found that to approach God *with others* added depth and texture and colour to my personal prayer in a way no amount of solo prayer could have done. That is not to say that I abandoned private prayer. Rather, I learned that private prayer and shared prayer overlap, affect and feed one another.

The first of these prayer groups came into being when a number of people in our church fellowship began to express an interest in listening prayer. We had all worked through considerable pain and animosity to reach this stage; their suspicion of my prayer pilgrimage subsided; my bitterness against those who questioned what I was doing had been dealt with, ruthlessly, by God. The meeting of our paths was sweet.

Our mid-week church fellowship had grown: from a prayer meeting attended by seven people who met in the rectory lounge to seventy people who congregated in the church hall each week. They wanted teaching as well as the opportunity to pray. For an experimental period, therefore, we set in motion a variety of workshops: on evangelism, on Bible study, on the Holy Spirit, to name but a few. One option open to anyone who wanted to come was a workshop on prayer.

For an hour a week, a group of us explored together the basics of listening to God. Together we experimented with various ways of entering into stillness. We tried a number of bodily postures, had fun in discovering together that deep, rhythmical breathing acts as a kind of metronome in prayer, spent time writing in our prayer journals, and learned to meditate in the way I have described in this book: on creation and on God's Word.

To some of the group God gave the gift of contemplation. When the trial period was over, they were hungry for more. We would therefore meet for an occasional Quiet Day when the exploration into collective silence would continue. One Saturday, we travelled to Derbyshire to spend the day in the quietness of the Derbyshire hills. The day began with worship when we re-focused from the busyness of the week on to God. It continued with a meditation on the story of Bartimaeus, followed by an opportunity to walk or sit, to enjoy 'just being' amidst the splendour of God's creation: a rare treat for city dwellers. The day concluded with an opportunity for anyone who wished to to express to the others what God had been saying in the re-creative silence.

On another Saturday we visited a farm not far from our home. We ate in silence and learned the value of listening as someone read to us while we ate instead of indulging in ceaseless, superficial chatter. Together we meditated on the claim of Jesus: 'I am the vine'. In our prayer journals we recorded some of the insights we had gleaned. And we celebrated Christ's death together in a quiet service of Holy Communion.

It has been said that Communion is the peak of contemplation. Prepared as we were, that day, by hours of delicious, fruitful stillness, we certainly soared to new heights of silent, corporate praise and adoration after we had received the sacrament. The awareness of the mystery, the majesty, the humility and the generosity of the God who was ever drawing us to himself filled us with a deep and intense joy.

But just as I, personally, was finding that a Quiet Day was frustratingly short, so we as a group would separate after a Quiet Day conscious that we had been brought to the threshold of a banqueting room whose door must again bar us from the feast inside. For this reason, weekend retreats became a feature of our group prayer twice a year.

We would start the retreat on Friday night, continue in silence until Sunday afternoon, then return to our church in time for the evening service. These retreats always incorporated a number of ingredients: worship, stillness, teaching, mutual ministry, liturgical prayer and intercession. Sometimes we would use the guesthouse at Mount St Bernard Abbey, sometimes the guesthouse at the Convent of St Laurence in Belper. Both were equidistant from our home: a drive of some forty minutes, which we considered to be long enough for a weekend retreat.

The main aim of the retreat never varied: we wanted to meet God face to face, as a living reality, and to support one another in this pursuit for an encounter with the risen Lord. A secondary aim was to learn together how to pray 'with our mind in our heart', to borrow a phrase popular among contemplatives. In other words, we wanted to explore for ourselves the well-tried methods of listening we were reading about: methods which enabled others not simply to know the theory about God but to know him in depth.

The pattern rarely varied. On Friday evening we would

arrive in time for supper during which we would exchange news. Between supper and the short service of compline, we would unpack and prepare ourselves for the stillness to come. After compline we would meet but not talk. The grand silence had begun and we wanted to become a part of it.

I cannot speak for the others, but during this time, when almost always we sat in a circle in a room which was lit only by a large candle, I would begin to express to God what I hoped for from this time apart with him. Then I would place the spotlight, not on me and my hopes and my anxieties, but on to him. This half hour together became, for me, a time of de-location, the godly pause which Guy Brinkworth has described so well which is 'reminiscent of the hush of concentration of the high jumper or competition diver just before the supreme effort'.[1]

After breakfast on Saturday, we would meet to study some of the basic principles of prayer. On our first retreat, one of the monks at Mount St Bernard Abbey urged us, if we were serious about learning to listen to God, to take prayer seriously. Among the notes I scribbled in my prayer journal are the following facts which I return to time and time again:

* Guarantee God a certain time each day: five minutes in the morning, perhaps, and five minutes in the evening. Don't set your sights too high. You can always give God *more* time than you promised initially but if you earmark half an hour and manage only five minutes your listening will be drowned by guilt feelings.

* The most unselfish prayer is the prayer you pray when you least feel like it. Then you pray out of love for God, not because it appears to benefit you.

* The crucial time is when we are not formally

praying at all. True prayer must be integrated into
our life. There is something phoney about the
person who 'lives' in church but has a very bitter
tongue.

We would take time to respond to simple ground rules
like these and tease out what God was saying to each of us
personally in connection with our life of listening prayer.
We would spend part of the day reading: either the Bible or
a book about prayer, or both.

Bible meditation of one form or another always featured
on our programme and as the group became a cohesive
unit we learned to value these more and more.

I remember one Sunday morning in Belper when we
read together the account of the healing of the woman who
suffered from haemorrhaging for twelve years. We tried, at
first, to visualise the scene: the pressing crowd, the poverty-
stricken woman, and Jesus. We then tried to put ourselves
into the scene in the way I described in an earlier chapter:
to *become* the sick woman whose need to touch the hem of
Jesus's garment was so urgent. As much as our
imaginations allowed, each of us felt the hot, sweaty
bodies of the crowd jostle him and identified with the
desperation that woman must have felt; in our own time
and manner, each of us stretched out his hand and touched
the bottom of Jesus's robe. And each of us saw Jesus turn,
heard him ask that curious question, 'Who touched me?',
basked in his acceptance and approval, savoured his
living, loving presence and allowed ourselves to be drawn
to him by that magnetism of his which never ceases to
attract people to himself.

I have said that 'each of us' entered into the meditation
in this way. That is not quite accurate. One member of the
group, a housewife and mother, described to the group
rather tearfully that she had spent the entire meditation
carrying a sick friend to Jesus. When she heard other
members of the group relate how Jesus had touched and

spoken to them, she felt envious. She had been so busy interceding for another that she had not stopped to have her own needs touched by the Son of God. 'That's typical of my life at the moment,' she admitted. 'I'm so busy caring for others that I don't give Jesus a chance to care for me.'

As leader of the group, I asked her if she would like to be touched by Jesus. After all, there was still time. She confessed that she would like a fresh touch from God. Most of the group held her into the love of God quite silently but supportively. Two or three of us laid hands on her head and prayed, again quite silently, that she would take courage in both hands as the woman suffering from the haemorrhage had done, and reach out to touch the home-spun garment of Jesus for herself. She did. There was no emotionalism. There *was* deep-felt joy as we watched her strained face break into a peaceful smile and as we saw the tension in her body disappear; as we saw her relax. When this young woman opened her eyes she became aware of the group's love and told us what had happened in the silence: Jesus had turned to her and touched her. She had looked into his eyes and seen sensitivity, gentleness and compassion – not only for her friend, but for her. This prayer ministry had taken less than ten minutes but it had proved life-changing for this young mother.

We were not day-dreaming or playing the child's game 'let's pretend' in these times of meditation. No. To God a thousand years are but yesterday; he is the same yesterday, today and forever. It seems a valid use of the gospel narrative, therefore, to meet the incarnate Christ, not only in its pages, but with our imagination and our senses also. To see and hear and touch him who came that man might see and hear and touch him seems a most natural approach to the Bible, a valid way to cross the time-vault together.

I learned to value this group more and more. It was to them that I submitted some of my own listening so that they could test whether what I was hearing was from God or wishful thinking. It was with them, therefore, that I grew in confidence. And it was with them that I realised that, though I could listen to God on my own, listening to God in the context of a community brought a wholeness and wholesomeness which no amount of praying in isolation could bring. In the group I put down roots. We belonged. It was as though the group was rather like a womb in which our listening prayer gestated and matured and in which we grew as individuals also.

New discoveries

At one stage the group met monthly in my prayer room. On Saturday evenings we would go there to be still together for an hour to prepare ourselves for Sunday and to give one another support. In this way we became soul friends to one another. We discovered that Jesus's promise to be especially present to the twos and threes who met in his name was relevant for us. The sense of his presence and power seemed almost tangible at times.

As time went on, a whole new dimension of listening prayer unfolded for us. It would sometimes happen that one member of the group would ask for prayer for a particular decision which had to be made, or for a seemingly insoluble problem. We rarely discussed the situation. Instead, in our customary silence, we would hold the person and the expressed need to God. As we did so, we would find that very often first one member of the group, then another, would receive an insight in the form of a picture, a passage of scripture, a thought, or a prophecy. This began to happen so frequently that, as leader of the group, I encouraged individuals to share such insights so that the entire group could test the source of the listening to ensure that it came from God, and so that we could piece together the fragments to make up the whole picture. What emerged was fascinating. I remember an occasion when I asked the group to pray for me because I was unsure whether to undertake a particular piece of counselling. After a prolonged period of silence one person quoted a verse of scripture which had impressed itself on her mind while she was praying. Another gave a word of prophecy in which God seemed to be promising to bring the person to be counselled through great darkness into light. At this, one girl gasped. 'That makes sense of a picture I've been seeing in my mind but couldn't make sense of,' she said. 'The picture is of a large swimming pool. I've watched you, Joyce, dive into the deep end of the pool with another person. For some considerable time you were both lost to sight – presumably you were swimming under water. Then you emerged in a different part of the pool. You were both bathed in light.'

The result of this piece of listening was that I embarked on the counselling situation. The picture of the swimming pool, in particular, encouraged me when the person I was trying to help seemed to make little progress. But this dimension of listening fascinated me for another reason. It demonstrated to me, again, the value of the group. Alone, I hear the whisperings of the Spirit of God in mono only. With others, we have the capacity to hear in stereo. On my own, I am capable of detecting only minute fragments of the whole purpose of God. But many pairs of ears pick up other fractions of God's vision. When we respect and learn from each other, we can put together our gleanings and gain a far more accurate impression of what God is trying to communicate.

Moving on
I said in an earlier chapter that God is always moving us on, that change for the Christian is an inevitability. One winter we became increasingly conscious that the group had fulfilled its function: we had served our apprenticeship in collective listening; it was time now to move back into the mainstream of the church. God would give us others with whom we would work in listening prayer.

I found it hard to disband the group. Once again I was forced to learn the lesson of detachment: to accept God's good gifts when he gives them but to be willing, when the time is ripe, to surrender them, trusting that what he removes with one hand, he replenishes with the other.

Looking back, I see one reason why the group had to break up. We could have become a ghetto. But God wanted us to leaven the lump of the fellowship. Today, members of that original listening group are teaching others to listen to God and are heavily involved in a listening ministry; four of them are Elders in our church – essentially a group which sets itself the task of listening to God; others lead 'link groups' (our term for house fellow-ships), others are members of the music group which leads the worship of the church but leans heavily on listening to God. Though we never meet today as we used to in the old days, the oneness between us has never been broken: we value one another, respect one another in a whole variety of ways, not least in the ministry of listening and intercessory prayer.

All kinds of listening

Since those early days of group listening, I have enjoyed a rich and varied diet of listening to God with others, and the learning has been enlightening.

On one occasion I visited a Greek Orthodox monastery where, for three days, I joined in the rhythm of prayer practised by the monks and nuns who live there. The special feature of this monastery, for me, was the use these people made of what is known as 'The Jesus prayer', a prayer which consists of the words, 'Lord Jesus Christ, Son of God, have mercy on us.'

For two hours every morning and two hours every evening, the community meet in the chapel to pray. They use these words and these only: 'Lord Jesus Christ, Son of God, have mercy on us.' As I prepared to visit this monastery, I feared that to recite this prayer would be nothing more than vain repetition. What I found as I joined in the prayer with these men and women was that, for four hours each day, I was listening to God on a profound level. I cannot speak for the others who participated in this prayer cycle, but, for me, I became acutely aware of two realities: the holiness of God and my own innate sinfulness. In one sense, this was not new. In another sense, it *was* new because of the manner in which I 'saw' the mystery and the 'otherness' and the glory of God and because of the manner in which I became equally conscious of my own nothingness before him. The fact that I am nothing, he is everything, and yet he loves me, hit home to me in a new and powerful way.

The music in this particular monastery conveyed to me more powerfully than any other music I have ever heard the fact of God's unending love. At various points in the day – before and after meals and during the communion service in particular – the entire community would break into unaccompanied, six-part harmony. It was not frothy, pseudo-praise but a plaintive, compelling form of communication which helped to quench my insatiable thirst to be filled with the love of God.

When it comes to the artistry of 'wasting time' with God – contemplating him for who he is and what he has done – I still find this comes more easily and readily in the context of a group. I have just returned from a convent where, on my retreat, I rested in God after a particularly hectic conference. There, in the convent, morning by morning after the communion service, I knelt with the sisters and dropped into the kind of silence where each of us was captivated by the love of Christ: where we were privileged, once again, to be lost in wonder, love and praise. Exhausted as I was, I doubt whether I could have managed this alone. But in this silence, supported by others, Christ came. I heard him. And rejoiced.

Chapter 19

Some Results of Listening to God

Whenever I close my eyes in an attempt to listen attentively to the sounds around, I am amazed at the mixture of noises which I had failed to hear until that moment: the humming of the fly, the hoot of the owl, the final faint song of the chaffinch, the creak of a chair. Similarly, whenever I tune into God's still, small voice the medley of experiences he gives astounds me. I can never anticipate beforehand what he will say or how he will act. What I can foretell is that whatever he gives will be worthwhile.

Early on in my prayer pilgrimage, I discovered that listening to God did not necessarily result in mystical experiences. Often, it was not other-worldly at all. Rather, it was a deeply practical affair.

I remember an occasion when the concept of listening to God seemed strange and new. While I was praying the words, 'Ring Valerie' kept pounding through my brain. Valerie was a close friend who lived eighty miles from my home. Feeling rather foolish, I telephoned. Valerie gasped when she heard my voice. We had not made contact for several months. 'What made you ring tonight?' she asked. 'Pam's here with me. Her husband died suddenly last night and I don't know what to say to her. She's just been saying, "I'd love to talk to Joyce." Will you speak to her?'

Pam was a mutual friend. She had expressed care for me after my father died. Now God gave me the privilege of drawing alongside her in her bereavement.

On another occasion, a young married couple came to me for counselling. For several years they had tried to start a family. When the wife failed to conceive they both subjected themselves to the necessary tests. These tests revealed that the husband was infertile. Should they adopt a child? Should they follow the advice they had been given and conceive a child with A.I.D.?

While they talked about their disappointment and moral dilemma, the Holy Spirit of God seemed to whisper the words, 'Pray for a miracle' in my spiritual ears. I had never prayed for a miracle baby before and was not sure that my faith would stretch that far. But the voice persisted so eventually I asked, 'Has it ever occurred to you that God might want to perform a miracle and give you a baby by natural means?'

The wife's face lit up. She, too, had sensed that this might be God's answer to their problem. The husband was uncertain. 'Supposing we pray and nothing happens?'

By this time the conviction in me was so strong that I suggested the husband borrowed the combination of his wife's faith and the little I could muster and we prayed that God would give them the gift of a child.

Six months later, the phone rang. I know the husband well and recognised his voice: 'Joyce! I've got something to tell you. My wife's pregnant.'

Thomas Merton once wrote:

Meditation has no point and no reality unless it is firmly rooted in *life*. Without such roots, it can produce nothing but the ashen fruits of disgust, *acedia*, and even morbid and degenerate introversion, masochism, dolorism, negation.[1]

And Richard Foster adds:

Often meditation will yield insights that are deeply

practical, almost mundane. There will come instruction on how to relate to your wife or husband, on how to deal with this sensitive problem or that business situation. More than once I have received guidance on what attitude to have when lecturing in a college classroom. It is wonderful when a particular meditation leads to ecstasy, but it is far more common to be given guidance in dealing with ordinary human problems.[2]

The practical nature of listening to God prompted me to keep these questions in my mind when I prayed:

* What is God saying?

* What is God giving to *me personally?*

* What is God asking me to take from this time with him into my world: to my husband, my children, my colleagues, my friends, my neighbours?

Just as Jesus's times alone with the Father overflowed to enrich the lives of the disciples, indeed of the entire world, so I wanted to avoid a me-centredness in my listening: to ensure that listening became the launching pad for more effective service and incisive ministry instead of degenerating into a bless-me club with a membership of one.

Praise, wonder
But listening to God need not be earthbound. It can transport one into worship, praise and adoration.

I recall an evening when I was meditating on the resurrection of Jesus. John's gospel lay open on the floor at my feet. I read chapter 20 as slowly as I could applying my senses to the unfolding scene. So I watched Mary steal to the sepulchre in the grey darkness of pre-dawn. I sensed her dismay as she saw, not the sealed tomb, but a yawning hole where the stone should have been. I heard her run to alert Peter and John, observed their race to the grave and, in my imagination, I went with Peter into the belly of the rock. I, too, saw the strips of linen lying there, 'the burial cloth that had been around Jesus's head. The cloth was folded up by itself, separate from the linen' (John 20:7).

And I gazed from the neat piles of linen to John who had crept quietly into the sepulchre. As wonder spread across his face and as he worshipped, my heart leapt with joy. I fell on my face and worshipped the resurrected Lord, not from any sense of duty, but with well-springs of praise which rose from somewhere deep inside me.

Pain

But just as listening to God can elicit paeans of praise so it can plunge the person at prayer into a deep and terrible pain. When this first happened to me and prayer triggered off uncontrollable weeping, I wondered what was happening. Now, I think I understand.

When we stand before God and tune into him, we pick up some of the heart-break he feels for a needy world. In this way God gives us the privilege of 'knowing him' and entering into the 'fellowship of his sufferings', to use the language of St Paul.

As I write this chapter a series of news bulletins on the radio has triggered off this inner weeping within me. Four young Buckinghamshire schoolboys were swept off the rocks at Land's End by a huge wave two days ago. Their bodies have not yet been found but they are presumed dead. News percolates through that the town in which they lived is in a deep state of shock. When I pray, my heart goes out to the mourning parents, the dazed pupils and the staff of the school.

This, I believe, is more than one mother empathising with another. It is an identification with the sorrow in God's heart as he contemplates human suffering. I do not understand why one tragedy can affect me in this way while another can leave me cold. What I do know is that in prayer I must hold this pain into the healing hands of

Christ so that his compassion and man's heartache can meet and be matched. This is the solemn responsibility of the person of prayer.

This weeping sometimes creeps up on us in curious ways. Just before I mapped out the outline for this chapter, a friend called to see me. He is a schoolteacher, a person God is drawing into listening prayer. He spelt out the horror he felt as he watched certain pupils in his school fight one another physically, just like little tigers. 'It hurts even to think about it,' he admitted. 'I don't understand why they want to be so cruel to each other.' I suggested that his inner turmoil and pain might have found a mooring in his heart for a purpose: because God wants him to weep and groan in prayer, not just for the situation at school, but because peace in the world has been pillaged, because in the world at large strife sets man against man on a bigger scale than this school scene.

Resting

Just as listening to God can produce pain and heartbreak, so it can result in a delicious resting in God. Thomas Merton puts this well when he describes the condition of 'resting in him whom we have *found*, who loves us, who is near to us, who comes to us to draw us to himself'.[3]

I recall the relief that has filled me on a number of occasions when I have come to prayer, weary but wanting to listen, and God's invitation has come so clearly: 'Don't talk. Just rest.' And I nestle in his arms and enjoy being held.

Re-creation

Listening to God, when the hearing prompts obedience, is always a re-creating experience. This may not be the re-creation of the comfortableness and contentment I have just described. To listen to God might mean to change. In God we are always on the move. He calls us from deep to deep. He requires us to be in his hands as clay submits to the hands of the potter. Those hands re-mould and re-shape us and the experience may be far from comfortable. As we listen he shows us how he wants these changes to take place.

Many pages of my prayer journal remind me of the way God put his finger on areas of my life and showed how they cripple me or distort his image.

I once expressed hatred of someone who had hurt me. God challenged me. The real reason for the hatred was that my pride had been wounded because friendship with me was a lower priority on this person's list than it used to be. God forced me, too, to face my jealousy. 'Pride and jealousy are sins to be confessed,' the Holy Spirit whispered, 'not rights to cling on to.' He gave me no peace until this sinful rubble was tipped out at the foot of the cross.

Sometimes the changes God wanted to bring about in my life took years rather than minutes. For months, pages of my prayer journal were devoted to the anger and frustration which poisoned my life and which stemmed from the growing tensions in our marriage.

In prayer I would whine to God about my husband: 'It really feels as though he doesn't care about me at all ... How little is his understanding and how very limited his compassion.' In prayer I would throw down the gauntlet and challenge God to change my husband so that the quality of our marriage could improve. In prayer I would pour out the self-pity that filled me to the brim: 'There's a big part of me, Lord, which is tired of trying, weary of forgiving, exhausted with the agony of gingerly putting my nose out of my hedgehog prickles only to have it stepped on again.'

And in prayer, God would come to me, hear me out, absorb my bitterness, touch my bruised and battered heart, and gently but persistently show me, not where David needed to change, but where *I* must change. Comments like this recur in my journal: 'And yes! I hear your voice again. Forgive! Not just seven times but seventy times seven.'

In addition, God would give clear, specific directions. On a day when my prayer journal reads like the ranting of a petulant child, the instructions God gave me read like a letter from a marriage counsellor:

* Take your own advice to others seriously: *listen* to David and his needs.

* Make time to be with him. You haven't done that for a whole week.

* Don't try to read his mind. Clarify what he really does feel about you and current circumstances. Make time for this clarification to take place.

* Look at the tensions in your marriage carefully. Learn from them. See where you must grow. Let them show you where you need healing. Let them highlight where sin stains the relationship. Respond to the challenge: change.

By God's grace we both changed so that the sharing of our lives today is more mutually fulfilling and fun-filled than it has ever been. Painful though it was at the time, I look back with gratitude at the patient surgical skills with which the Holy Spirit operated on me to break me, re-create me and to rid me of spiritual diseases in the hospital of prayer. Through this I learned that God gives the gift of listening prayer not primarily to provide us with warm feelings towards him, though he does enrich our lives in this way, but to impress on us the need to grow. Listening prayer may not give us cosiness. It will bring us into wholeness, the *shalom* which is the integration of body, mind and spirit.

The dark night of the soul

One of the methods God uses to bring about this inner harmony in some people is an experience which is sometimes called 'the dark night of the soul'. This phrase describes the phases of the spiritual journey when the senses no longer pick up the felt presence of Christ but seem to be conscious, instead, only of nothingness. During this winter of the senses God seems to be, not present and attentive and loving, but completely absent. Thomas Merton refers to this experience often and describes it variously: 'spiritual inertia, inner confusion, coldness, lack of confidence'.[4] 'What at first seemed rosy and rewarding suddenly comes to be utterly impossible. The mind will not work. One cannot concentrate on anything. The imagination and the emotions wander away.'[5]

In my prayer diary, I record the pain and bewilderment which the apparent absence of God brings: 'I ache for fellowship with you, Lord, but you seem so silent. You, whom this time last week I held and loved and cherished seem to have gone away again. Come, Lord Jesus, with healing hands...'

What I am referring to here is not simply an absence of warm feelings in prayer but something more profound than that: a definite sense that God had vanished, even abandoned me.

The first time I encountered the horror of this seeming separation from God, I was on retreat. Faced with four whole days of solitude, instead of the sense of anticipation which normally filled me at such times, I was seized with a sudden, severe sense of panic, even fear. I dreaded the moment when I must cross the threshold into silence.

In the convent where I had retreated to pray lived a nun who knew me well. In her I confided: 'Please pray for me. I don't know what's happening but I'm terrified of going into silence. God seems to have disappeared. He just isn't there any more and I'm left with this awful emptiness.'

She smiled and seemed quite unperturbed by the nature

of the problem. Friend and confidante as she was, she prayed with me and for me and opened my eyes to the fact that in the school of prayer this particular seminar is a training ground for those who would graduate in the art of listening to God. In the first place, it increases our longing for God.

This became my experience. The darkness which crept over me in the convent on that occasion caused me to shudder and draw back, but it drew from me a call for Christ which came from the very depths of my being and which I experienced as a near-physical pain. It set me on a search for him which was both urgent and full of anguish. Was it, perhaps, the kind of search which sent Mary to the tomb very early on that Easter Day, full of longing to find the love which had been snatched away so suddenly? Was it reminiscent of the anxious hurt of the bride for her bridegroom in the Song of Songs? (3:1-2). Certainly, it seemed an identification with the pain David expresses so poignantly:

> As the deer pants for streams of water,
>   so my soul pants for you, O God.
> My soul thirsts for God, for the living God.
>   When can I go and meet with God?' (Ps. 42:1-2).

And it echoed his cry of bewilderment: 'Why have you forgotten me?' (Ps. 42:9).

But it did more than expose my genuine desire for God. It sharpened my spiritual ears. God seemed to be hiding. But he had promised never to leave me or forsake me. He must, therefore, be there – somewhere. My spiritual antennae quivered with eagerness and alertness to detect even the faintest sign of his presence.

Meanwhile the nothingness which engulfed me forced me into some necessary sifting. As I thought about my normal programme of priorities – the people I spent time with, the activities I enjoyed, the work I found so fulfilling

– I recognised the truth of the situation that in comparison with Christ and his presence the best the world can offer is but a mean and paltry offering. Thus the world lost more of its lure and lustre and what the mystics describe as the *capax Dei*, the capacity for God, increased. And deep down this was what I wanted. If this yawning emptiness was the enlargement of my inner capacity for God, then I would welcome these desert experiences. The intermingling of cautious trust and longing expressed in a prayer I once heard became *my* prayer:

> You, oh lord, are the thing that I long for
> And yet
>   I'm not sure that I can bear the emptiness that this
>   longing will involve
> If I really long for you then there will be no room for
>   the clutter
>   of a lot of other longings...
>
> I must be hollowed out
> To become a capacity for you.
> I shrink from the pain that that will involve
> But I must needs feel the poverty of my emptiness
> And my poverty meets with your giving in the silence
>   of lovers.

And, of course, when he saw that the time was ripe, God overwhelmed me once more with his felt presence. Meanwhile, having dispensed with the debris within, I had been enlarging the reservoir into which he could pour the life-giving waters of his Spirit's loving, invigorating presence. And when the 'tremendous lover' did return, the wave of joy which broke on the shore of my soul gave birth to a song of heart-felt thanksgiving and relief. And I realised I had learned another valuable lesson: that I must not depend on feelings nor dictate to God *how* he will appear to me. If he has spoken in a certain way on one occasion, I must not expect that necessarily he will visit me in that way a second time. I must allow God to be God. And I must recall that he is not here to meet my neurotic needs nor to kow-tow to my whims and fancies. He is here to transform me into his likeness. The work of God's Spirit is to grow me up into the likeness of Christ. Just as one third of our earthly existence is spent in physical darkness, night, so God in his wisdom ordains that from time to time my prayer life must work a few night-shifts also. The mystery is, as the psalmist reminds us, that the darkness is not dark to him: 'The night will shine like the day' (Ps. 9:12).

I learned, too, that this darkness is a relative phen-omenon. As someone once explained it to me, 'When you've been looking into the sun, you turn round and everything seems dark. Similarly, when you've been gazing at Jesus, everything else lies in his shadow.'

Thomas Merton makes the claim that these night times of the senses increase in frequency as time goes on, that there is a sense in which they can be taken as signs of progress provided the pray-er does not give up but determines to respond to the challenge, refuses to view this hollowness as spiritual doom or punishment for sin, but sees it, rather, for what it really is: the opportunity for growth.

Speaking personally, I still shudder when prayer dries up on me, when I listen and hear nothing, when I yearn for God and find emptiness, but I am learning, slowly, that the darkness is but the shadow of his hand, silence but the herald of his call, and nothingness the space prepared for the return of never-ending love.

As we listen to God, the pendulum swings from practicalities to ecstasies, from joy to pain and back again. But always our aim in prayer is to listen to the persistent tick-tock of his voice. When we do this, others take notice, benefit from the overflow, and give glory to God. As the pagan Queen of Sheba put it, reflecting on Solomon's in-

touchness with God: 'Praise be to the Lord your God, who
has delighted in you' (2 Chr. 9:8).

Chapter 20

Pray as you Can

Early on in my prayer pursuit, I heard a wise maxim: 'Pray as you can, not as you can't.' In other words, pray and listen to God in a manner which holds meaning for you personally. Beware of falling into the trap of aping another person's prayer style. For the would-be listener to God this advice is priceless.

All kinds of components make up the complete listening package, as we have seen. Not everyone will gain access through each component. To some, God will communicate his purposes in one way, to others he will reveal his plans in a completely different manner. At different times and in different places he may communicate to the same person in a whole variety of ways. As we noted in chapter nineteen, we must allow God to be God, to take the initiative as he will. Our responsibility is to be ever-ready to receive his transmissions as and when he sends them.

I have tried to demonstrate, through the pages of this book, some of the ways in which I have grown in my understanding and experience of listening to God. Even so, I am conscious that I have not yet 'arrived', but still have much to learn.

Although I consider myself to be no more than an undergraduate where the study of listening prayer is concerned, I propose to devote this final chapter to a question I am asked frequently by fellow seekers: 'How can *I* learn to listen to God more effectively?'

Know your background

My first response to this question is to suggest that you take stock of your spiritual background.

Speaking personally, I dislike the man-made labels we use frequently to compartmentalise ourselves and others and I try, whenever possible, to resist the words 'evangelical', 'contemplative', or 'charismatic'. However, there are occasions when such words form a convenient shorthand and to this shorthand I shall resort in this chapter.

If you are an evangelical, and you are coming to the end of this book thirsting to hear God's voice more adequately, the first thing to do is to be grateful for the tools which your background has, in all probability, placed at your disposal already: a thorough working knowledge of and love of the Bible.

I have shown elsewhere in this book that informed biblical thinking is an essential component of listening prayer. Indeed it is the touchstone of all our listening.

Having said that, it would be foolish to imply that the Christian from an evangelical background has at his fingertips *all* the tools which the skilled listener needs. Very often he has not. Some evangelicals are rather like the bee I watched the other day. It perched on the outer petals of a peach-coloured rose, crawled right round the perimeter, presumably appreciated its fragrance, but flew away without bothering to penetrate the heart of the rose where the pollen collects.

What I watched reminded me of the evangelical I had talked to a few hours earlier. He and I were attending the same Christian conference. He clamoured for more biblical teaching, insisting that his mind must be fed. Yet in a quiet moment, he admitted to me that he was living promiscuously and was certain that this was all right.

If we would learn to listen to God more effectively, we evangelicals must learn that listening to God involves much more than cerebral activity. It demands a living response: obedience. And it demands attentiveness to God at many levels: intellectual, emotional, spiritual, volitional. In other words, the challenge to the evangelical may well be to tune into God with his emotions, his will and his spirit as well as with his mind. As Jesus put it, love for God involves a whole-hearted dedication of heart, mind, soul and strength. Until we give this, we miss the very heart of the gospel and tune out much of what God is attempting to say.

The evangelical Christian who is anxious to listen to God more attentively may have other disciplines to master. We in evangelical circles are not very experienced in keeping quiet. We have to *learn* to 'be still', to know that God is God. We have to learn 'to be' and not necessarily to achieve. We may even need to be persuaded that God is prepared to speak to us in unexpected ways, through nature, other people, our imagination, as well as through his revealed Word, the Bible.

There was a second bee on the peach-coloured rose I mentioned earlier. This one also crawled round the perimeter of the flower, then it pushed its way among the petals and hummed as it carried its collection of pollen away in its pocket. For the evangelical Christian, listening to God can be as productive as that. He has already landed on the right flower. If he will learn to value and adopt the insights of others, if he will learn to meditate as well as study, feel as well as think, he can discover far more to listening than he formerly believed was possible.

The contemplative

The contemplative Christian who asks this same question, 'How can *I* listen to God more effectively?' also has cause to thank God for the richness of his spiritual heritage. In all probability he has been schooled in the art of stillness.

And such stillness is a prerequisite for listening to the still, small voice of God as Ladislas Orsy reminds us: 'Discernment requires contemplative persons, well-versed in finding God's presence by instinct. A gentle sensitivity to the gentle movements of grace is necessary to the point of being an indispensable condition. Without it there is no wholeness in discernment.'[1] The contemplative may well have achieved a heightened awareness of the presence of Christ, particularly in the communion and in the community. He may also have become quite skilled in reading some of God's signs, seeing him in nature, or in the face of a child, or feeling him in the force of the wind.

But just as the evangelical has to learn that listening to God goes beyond the narrow sphere of reading words, so the contemplative, in refining the art form of listening to God, may need to turn back from mere signs and the teaching of the church to the scriptures – to study them, to become conversant with them. The desert fathers and teachers of prayer have passed on much wise counsel and it is sheer folly to ignore the wisdom they have imparted down the ages. Nevertheless, if we would know the mind of God we must heed the Word of God. *It* must become our chief delight. *It* must lodge in our hearts and minds. *It* must govern our thinking. If we do not know what the Word of God contains we may be sinning against God without ever intending to do so.

We contemplatives may face other challenges also. God is always on the move, as we have seen. If we cling to fossilised forms of worship, if we are frightened of departing from the rubric, if we are suspicious of every movement of the Spirit which we cannot explain, we will bolt the door on God and shut out his voice. We contemplatives may need to be persuaded to believe that Jesus says of himself 'I AM', not 'I WAS'. He is living and active and communicating today in supernatural ways and unless we accept this, his multi-layered communication will fall on deaf hearts and minds. Moreover, we may fail to discover the 'new thing' which God is always creating.

Just as the evangelical may find himself with unexpected avenues to explore, so the contemplative faces a life of fruitful exploration if he is prepared for the challenge which listening brings in its wake: to study, to re-evaluate, to discern every movement of the wind of the Spirit.

The charismatic

The charismatic asking the question, 'How can *I* listen to God?', similarly, has a certain head start and severe limitations.

We charismatics need no persuading that God is at work today, changing people's lives in a supernatural way. We have seen it for ourselves. We rejoice. We want to be open to everything God wants to do and to say.

But this very enthusiasm can be our greatest handicap. Our spontaneity can be the greatest obstacle we bring to the work of listening to God. For God says, in effect, 'Shut up!' 'Listen!' And shutting up is a discipline in which we do not excel!

The charismatic Christian whose hunger to hear God is real can learn from the contemplative to stop talking, stop clapping, stop praising for a while. And listen. In the stillness all that is phoney is stripped away. In this stillness authentic adoration is born which can later be expressed in exuberant praise if need be. In this stillness the desire for the spectacular is replaced by a deeper desire to know God for himself alone, not for anything he can do.

And we charismatics, like the contemplative, must follow the example of Jesus and steep ourselves in the scriptures. We must sharpen our thinking powers and use them. Unless we do so, we may find ourselves making pronouncements in the name of Christ which run counter to the Word of God. To do so is serious. God cannot contradict himself. If we are to speak out in the name of

God, we must make it our responsibility to know what the Word of God contains.

Like the evangelical and the contemplative, the charismatic brings certain strengths to listening prayer but if the gift is to be perfected, for most of us, a great deal of hard work lies ahead.

To any Christian who, with genuineness, asks the question, 'How can *I* listen to God more effectively?' the way ahead is plain, in my view. We must recognise the skills already entrusted to us by God, give thanks for them, and use them efficiently. Then, instead of falling into the trap of *criticising* Christians from other traditions, we shall begin to ask, not, 'How can I prove that they're wrong?' but rather, 'What can I learn from them?' We shall not expect to agree with everything a person from another tradition believes in or stands for. Nevertheless, if we are to obey the command of Jesus, to love them as he loves them, we shall learn to accept and value all that God is doing in them and, in the area of listening to God, to take on board disciplines which clearly assist them in the task in hand: to listen to God with accuracy. In this way, too, we shall be captivated continually by the expanding vision of God which creeps over our horizon. We shall realise, in the language of J. B. Phillips, that for all our life so far, our God has been too small.

Know yourself

Just as the would-be listener can learn to discern his strength and limitations by acknowledging the insights his background has provided and areas in which his particular fellowship is deficient, so the would-be listener can improve his ability to listen to God by becoming aware of his personality.

The analyst, Carl Jung, divided people into personality types: the extrovert and the introvert. One is not better, more mature, than the other; they are different. He went further and subdivided each of these personality types in four ways according to the manner in which they approached life: through sensation, intuition, thinking and feeling.

There is great value in admitting to yourself where your chief bias lies because, in all probability, you will hear God speaking to you in certain ways which fit your personality.

For example, the extrovert who is a thinking person is more likely to hear the voice of God through the study of the Bible, the reading of commentaries, the evaluation of doctrines and the clarifying of theological positions than through nature and the imagination. The introvert who is a thinking person, on the other hand, will seek to hear God through Bible *meditation*, the slow reading of scripture, devotional reading. One is not better than the other. They are different.

Similarly, the extrovert who is motivated to a high degree by sensations may seek a fresh touch from God by attending celebration services. By watching or participating in spiritual dance, drama or the singing of scripture choruses, he will tune in to God. The introvert, who is governed by sensations, on the other hand, will seek God's presence in the calm of a convent, in the quiet of contemplation, or a country walk, or in the peace of a place preserved for prayer. One is not better than the other. They are different. The extrovert will seek to hear God outside of himself because, by definition, the extrovert turns outwards. The introvert, on the other hand, will seek attentiveness to God by paying attention to the world within because, by definition, the introvert feeds the inner world. One is not better than the other. They are different.

The challenge to those of us who would listen to God is to 'pray as we can'; to recognise the particular bias which we bring to the discipline of listening because of our personality, to start from there and then to move outside of these self-limiting boundaries to explore methods of listening which are valued by people with personality types which are different from our own.

Let me explain what I mean. I am an introvert. If I moved within the restricted sphere of my personality type, I would restrict myself to silence, Bible meditation, slow reading of scripture, contemplating God in nature, hearing God with the vividness of my imagination. But I married an extrovert and early on in our marriage we set ourselves the task of learning to find value in what the other enjoyed. My husband loves services of celebration, intellectual discussions and drama. Over the years, while I have been seeking to discover why he values such things, I have discovered that God speaks to me, not only in ways I would expect as an introvert, but in ways I would expect him to speak to my extrovert husband also. This not only enhances my listening, it brings a sense of completeness and wholeness. In the same service I can now drop into the stillness of the presence of God *and* praise him with my tambourine!

Know your Lord

It is not enough to know our background and know ourselves. We must know our Lord as well. Jesus has a wonderful way of making his presence known to all kinds of personality types and to people from a variety of backgrounds.

Think of the Resurrection appearances of Jesus, for example. Early in the morning, on the first Easter Day, Jesus appeared to Mary around whose neck we might hang the label 'contemplative', or 'introvert'. While Mary wept out her grief at the mouth of the empty tomb, Jesus appeared to her. He gave her the luxury her heart pined for: a long, leisurely opportunity to gaze at the Master she adored; the opportunity to drink in the Lord's one loving word to her, 'Mary', her own name.

Or think of the disciples who tramped the road which stretches from Jerusalem to Emmaus. Perhaps these two were extroverts: thinking types. As Jesus drew alongside them in their grief, his approach was quite different from his meeting with Mary. He appealed, not to their emotions, but to their minds. He expounded the scriptures, opened the eyes of their understanding, and rebuked them for neglecting to use their thinking powers. And by the end of the journey they heard him. In meeting them in their need he had used a language they could understand.

Think, too, of Peter, the extrovert who reacted to situations rather than responding to them after careful thought. For Peter, Jesus performed a miracle. After Peter's abortive all-night fishing trip, Jesus pointed out where a massive shoal of fish could be found. And as though that was insufficient, Jesus took his disconsolate disciple on one side and reinstated him, assuring him in a language Peter could interpret, that his denial of his Master was forgiven.

These different people with different personality types and different needs had one thing in common. They encountered the living Lord Jesus in a way which was unique to them.

While I have been writing this book, the conviction in me has deepened that this living Lord Jesus still yearns to communicate: through his Word, through his people, through circumstances, through nature, and through a whole variety of ways which only a creative God could devise. While I have been writing this book, I have also become increasingly aware that large numbers of Christians in the world today are crying out for a deeper encounter with this Creator God. It is my prayer that what I have written may contribute in some small way to a matching of the two: that this book may, perhaps, become a bridge on which a communicating God and some listening Christians encounter one another in love.

For me, as I have said, fasting, prayer journals, Quiet Days and retreats, Bible study, Bible meditation, slow reading and the contemplation of nature have all contributed to my growth in listening to God. But that does not necessarily mean that each of these will feature in *your* life in a significant way. I repeat: 'Pray as you can, not as you can't'.

The young mother may long for a Quiet Day but be unable to shed her responsibilities for such a luxury. Five minutes of silence will be bliss indeed. A family living in cramped conditions could not hope for a prayer room. A person living in the inner city may see little sign of God in creation.

Not everyone will take on board all the aids to listening I have mentioned all of the time. Some will help and encourage others at different phases of their life. My advice is: experiment. See what works for you. If a particular method of listening seems to be an asset in refining your ability to listen to God, use it. If it does not help, leave it on one side without any sense of guilt or shame.

Five minutes for God

But be disciplined. Christians who are serious in their desire to listen to God embark on a journey. It is full of surprises which make of it an adventure. But as I have already hinted, it is an ascent, a climb, hard work. Most of us can reserve a chair in a corner as a prayer place if we are disciplined. Most of us can carve out five minutes each day for God if we are disciplined. Most of us can learn to weave prayer into our chores if we are disciplined. Many of us *can* fast and even manage a Quiet Day if we are disciplined. And without discipline we shall never learn to listen. That is partly why we need each other.

God is always more anxious to speak than we are to listen. Speaking personally, the awareness of this fact spurs me on.

As I write, propped up in my prayer corner is Ulrich Schaffer's book, *Into Your Light*. On one page, the contemplative camera has captured the underside of a leaf, photographing the web of veins which give it life. On the facing page, the poet records his response to God's invitation to course through his life in like manner:

> I sense your drive
> To flow through me
> Into the smallest blood vessels
> Because you want to be my heartblood
> In all the passages of my life
> And you want to become visible in the leaves
> And the fruit that I bear.
>
> Spread out in me
> Press forward, penetrate, pierce and flow
> Even if, at times,
> I want to repeal this invitation
> Being afraid of your ways in me.
>
> Circulate in me
> Change and renew
> Because I know
> That only your Spirit
> Can bring real life and fruit.[2]

As one who is spiritually full but never satisfied, who has been found but still searches, who has heard but still waits in listening love, I, too, echo that prayer. Spread out in me, Lord Jesus, until I see you face to face.

Notes

Preface
1. Gerard Manley Hopkins: *The Wreck of the Deutschland*
2. C. S. Lewis: *The Four Loves*. Fontana, 1963, p 128

Chapter 1
1. Francis Thompson: *The Hound of Heaven*. Mowbrays, pp 4–6

Chapter 2
1. John Powell: *He Touched Me*. Argus, 1974, p 70
2. Ibid, p 71
3. Ibid, p 74; p 77
4. C. S. Lewis: *Surprised by Joy*. Fontana, 1962, pp 173–4

Chapter 3
1. Catherine de Hueck Doherty: *Poustinia*. Fountain, 1975, p 20
2. Ibid, p 21
3. Robert Llewellyn: *Prayer and Contemplation*. Fairacres, 1975, p 29

Chapter 4
1. James Borst: *Contemplative Prayer*. Ligoun Publications, 1979, p 43. (A revised version of *A Method of Contemplative Prayer*.)
2. Robert Llewellyn: *Prayer and Contemplation*. Fairacres, 1975, p 33

3. See, for example, Ezekiel 2:1–2
4. See, for example, Psalms 88:9 and Job 11:13
5. For further information read *The Body at Prayer* by
    H. Caffarel. SPCK, 1978
6. James Borst: *A Method of Contemplative Prayer*. MHM,
    Asian Trading Corporation, 1973, p 11
7. W. Phillip Keller: *Solitude for Serenity and Strength*.
    Decision Magazine, August-September 1981, p 8

Chapter 5
1. James Borst: *A Method of Contemplative Prayer*. Asian
    Trading Corporation, 1974, p 12
2. Thomas Merton: *Contemplative Prayer*. DLT, 1973, p 13
3. Ibid, p 7
4. Ibid, p 8
5. Ibid, p 15 (italics mine)

Chapter 6
1. W. Phillip Keller: *Solitude for Serenity and Strength*.
    Decision Magazine, August-September 1981, p 8
2. Stephen Verney: *Into the New Age*. Fontana, 1976, p 90
3. Ibid, p 92
4. James Borst: *The Cloud of Unknowing*. Quoted *Con-
    templative Prayer*. Ligouri Publications, 1979, p 59
5. Dom Vitalis Lehodey. Quoted ibid, p 58
6. C. S. Lewis: *The Lion, the Witch and the Wardrobe*. Puffin
    1966 p 148
7. James Borst MHM: *A Method of Contemplative Prayer*.
    Asian Trading Corporation, 1974, p 18
8. Ibid, pp 18–19
9. Thomas Merton: *Contemplative Prayer*. DLT, 1973, p 115
10. Anon.: *The Cloud of Unknowing*. Penguin, 1977, p 51
11. Stephen Verney: *Into the New Age*. Fontana, 1976,
    pp 91–2

Chapter 7
1. J. I. Packer: *God's Thoughts*. IVP, 1981, p 39
2. David Watson: *Discipleship*. Hodder and Stoughton, 1981,
    p 149

Chapter 8
1. Michael Mitton: *The Wisdom to Listen*. Grove Pastoral Studies no 5, 1981, p 10
2. Richard Foster: *Meditative Prayer*. MARC Europe, 1983, p 3

Chapter 9
1. David Watson: *Discipleship*. Hodder and Stoughton, 1981, p 145
2. Herman Riffel: *Your Dreams: God's Neglected Gift*. Kingsway, 1984, p 9
3. Ibid, p 48

Chapter 10
1. Kallistos Ware: *The Orthodox Way*. Mowbrays, 1979, p 21
2. Billy Graham: *Angels: God's Secret Agents*. Hodder and Stoughton, 1975, pp 12–13
3. Ibid, pp 154–5
4. Anthony Bloom: *Taped Talk on a Quiet Day*, made privately, so unavailable to public.

Chapter 11
1. Charles de Foucauld
2. Quoted Kallistos Ware: *The Orthodox Way*. Mowbrays, 1979, p 54
3. See *Practising the Presence of God* by Brother Lawrence.
4. Quoted Kallistos Ware: *The Orthodox Way*. Mowbrays, 1979, p 4
5. Ulrich Schaffer: *Into your Light*. IVP, 1979, pp 43–4
6. John Powell: *He Touched Me*. Argus, 1974, p 79
7. Kallistos Ware: *The Orthodox Way*. Mowbrays, 1979 p 58

Chapter 12
1. Kallistos Ware: *The Orthodox Way*. Mowbrays, 1979, p 88
2. Keith Miller: *The Taste of New Wine*. A Word Paperback, 1970, p 93
3. David Watson: *One in the Spirit*. Hodder Christian Paperbacks, 1973, pp 90–1
4. David Watson: *Discipleship*. Hodder and Stoughton, 1981

Chapter 13

1. J. I. Packer: *Knowing God*. Hodder and Stoughton 1973 p 264
2. Thomas Merton: *Contemplative Prayer*. DLT, 1973, p 43
3. Ps. 119:16,162; 11; 15,27,48; 2,115,129; 13; 52; 97,99,148,94, 110,157
4. Francis Schaeffer: *The New Super-Spirituality*. Hodder and Stoughton, 1972, p24

Chapter 14

1. Quoted in *The Practice of Bible Meditation* by Campbell McAlpine, Marshalls, 1981, p 20
2. Ibid, p 20
3. J. I. Packer: *God's Words*. IVP, 1981, p 35
4. David Watson: *Discipleship*. Hodder and Stoughton, 1981, p 147
5. Campbell McAlpine: *The Practice of Bible Meditation*. Marshalls, 1981, p 75
6. M. Basil Pennington D.C.S.O.: *Centering Prayer*. Image Books, 1982, p 193
7. Richard Foster: *Meditative Prayer*. MARC Europe, 1983, pp 23-4

Chapter 15

1. Mother Mary Clare SLG – Talk on tape
2. Andre Louf: *Teach us to pray*. DLT, 1974
3. Henri J. Nouwen: *The Genesee Diary*. Image Books, 1981, p 14
4. Ibid, p 135
5. William Barclay: *The Gospel of Matthew* Vol. 2. Saint Andrew Press, 1975, p 60

Chapter 16

1. Guy Brinkworth, SJ: *Thirsting for God*. Mullan Press
2. Ibid, p 16
3. Ibid, p 12
4. Ibid, p 13

5. Quoted in *You* by Mark Link. Argus, 1976, p 53
6. Catherine de Hueck Doherty: *Pustinia*. Fountain, 1975, p 70
7. Ibid, p 93
8. Michel Quoist: *Prayers of Life*. Gill & Macmillan, 1966, pp 101–2
9. For suggestions of music to bring one into stillness, see Appendix
10. Kenneth Leech: *Soul Friend*. Sheldon Press, 1977, p 170
11. Quoted in *Soul Friend* by Kenneth Leech. Sheldon Press, 1977, p 41
12. Quoted Ibid, p 44
13. Quoted Ibid, Frontispiece
14. *Pray with ...* Bro. Kenneth CGA and Sister Geraldine Dss. CSA C10, 1977, p 15

Chapter 17

1. C. S. Lewis: *The Screwtape Letters*. Fontana, 1956, p 114
2. Richard Foster: *Celebration of Discipline*. Hodder and Stoughton, 1980, p 48

Chapter 18

1. Guy Brinkworth SJ: *Personal Renewal and Formal Prayer*. Convent of Mercy, 1970, p 32

Chapter 19

1. Thomas Merton: *Contemplative Prayer*. DLT, 1973, p 45
2. Richard Foster: *Celebration of Discipline*. Hodder and Stoughton, 1978, p 17
3. Ibid, p 32
4. Ibid, p 44
5. Ibid, p 44

Chapter 20

1. Ladislas M. Orsy: *Probing the Spirit*. Dimension Books, 1976, p 14
2. Ulrich Schaffer: *Into your Light*. IVP, 1979, p 29

Bibliography

The aim of this bibliography is to provide a list of some of the books whose insights on prayer have proved helpful to me personally. Like all books, they should be read with discretion. Their inclusion in this list does not mean that I agree totally with everything each author writes. In many instances I would take a different theological viewpoint from the author while, at the same time, valuing his/her teaching on the practice or meaning of prayer.

Author Unknown	*The Could of Unknowing*	Penguin Classics
Abishiktananda	*Prayer*	
Archbishop Anthony Bloom	*School of Prayer*	Libra
Archbishop Anthony Bloom	*Living Prayer*	Libra
Guy Brinkworth	*Personal Renewal and Formal Prayer*	Convent of Mercy
Guy Brinkworth	*Thirsting for God*	Mullan Press
Maria Boulding	*Marked for Life*	SPCK
James Borst MHM	*Contemplative Prayer*	Ligouri Publications
Ruth Burrows	*Before the Living God*	Sheed and Ward
Carlo Carretto	*In Search of the Beyond*	DLT
Carlo Carretto	*The God Who Comes*	DLT
Carlo Carretto	*Summoned by Love*	DLT
Carlo Carretto	*The Desert in the City*	DLT

Pierre de Caussade	*Self-abandonment to Divine Providence*	Fontana
Catherine de Hueck Doherty	*Poustinia*	Fountain
Edward Farrell	*Prayer is a Hunger*	The Hart Library
Richard Foster	*Celebration of Discipline*	Hodder and Stoughton
Richard Foster	*Meditative Prayer*	Marc Europe
Morton T. Kelsey	*The Other Side of Silence: A guide to Meditation*	SPCK
Thomas à Kempis	*The Imitation of Christ*	Lakeland
Brother Lawrence	*The Practice of the Presence of God*	Bagster
Kenneth Leech	*Soul Friend*	Sheldon Press
Kenneth Leech	*True Prayer*	Sheldon Press
C. S. Lewis	*The Screwtape Letters*	Fontana
C. S. Lewis	*Letters to Malcolm*	Fontana
Mark Link	*You*	Argus
Robert Llewelyn	*Prayer and Contemplation*	Fairacres
Robert Llewelyn	*Love Bade me Welcome*	DLT
Robert Llewelyn	*The Positive Role of distraction in prayer*	Fairacres
André Louf	*Teach us to Pray*	DLT
Ralph Martin	*Hungry for God*	Fontana

Mother Mary Clare SLG	*Learning to Pray*	Fairacres
Campbell McAlpine	*The Practice of Biblical Meditation*	Marshalls
Thomas Merton	*Contemplative Prayer*	DLY
Michael Mitton	*The Wisdom to Listen*	Grove Pastoral Series
Henri J. Nouwen	*With Open Hands*	Ava Maria Press
Henri J. Nouwen	*The Genessee Diary*	Image
Henri J. Nouwen	*Reaching Out*	Fount
J. I. Packer	*Knowing God*	Hodder and Stoughton
M. Basil Pennington OCSO	*Centering Prayer*	Image
John Powell	*He Touched Me*	Argus
Michel Quoist	*Prayers of Life*	Gill and Son
David R. Smith	*Fasting*	
Gilbert Shaw Fairacres	*A Pilgrim's Book of Prayers*	
Simon Tugwell	*Prayer: Living with God*	Veritas
Stephen Verney	*Into the New Age*	Fontana
J. Neville Ward	*Friday Afternoon*	Epworth
Kallistos Ware	*The Orthodox Way*	Mowbrays
David Watson	*Discipleship*	Hodder and Stoughton

Some of the music I use to bring me into silence

Music from Taize

Laudate:

Stay Here Jesus, Remember Me
Psalm 50 and Kyrie Eleison
Adoramus Te Domine
Venis Sancte Spiritus
Ubi Caritas
Salvator Mundi
Alleluia
Laudate Dominum

Resurrexit:

Dona la pace
Exaudi nos
Bleibet hier
O Christe Domine Jesu
O Lord, hear my prayer
Alleluia
Dona nobis pacem Domine

Music from St Aldate's Church, Oxford

King of Kings

Come let us worship our Redeemer
King of Kings
Father you are everything to me
Light shining in the darkness

Lord of Creation

Lay your burdens down
Within a quiet soul
We worship you

Music from St Michael-le-Belfry Church, York

Come and Worship:

For thou, O Lord
The King is among us
Glorify thy name
Jesus, Lord of all
Kyrie Eleison

With Thanksgiving:

Come Lord Jesus
Broken for me
Thou dost keep him
Jesus how lovely you are
Jesus is Lord

Peace with the Father

My peace
Jesus I give you

Piano Music

(From the tape: *Piano Moods:*)

Gymnopedie No. 1 – Satie
Claire de Lune – Debussy
Traumerei from Kinderscened Op. 15 – Schumann
Liebestraum No. 3 in Ab major – Liszt
Jesus, Joy of Man's Desiring – Bach

Beethoven: Piano Sonata no. 8 in C minor op. 13 Pathetique
Beethoven: Piano Sonata no. 14 in C sharp minor op. 27 no. 2 Moonlight.
Chopin Preludes

Music from The Vineyard

(From the tape: *You Are Here:*)

You are here
You are the vine
Open your eyes

(From the tape: *All the earth shall worship:*)

I Worship You
Alleluia

Music from the Fisherfolk

(From the record: *God's People Give Thanks:*)

Jesus I love you
Alleluia
My Jesus I love thee
Glory be to Jesus
Come to my marriage feast

Orchestral Music

Pachabel: Canon in D
Corelli: Christmas Concerto
Albinoni: Adagio in G minor for organ
Elgar: Enigma Variations Nimrod
Bach: Air on a G String
Vivaldi: The Four Seasons

(From the tape: *Reflections:*)

Theme from *Brideshead Revisited*
Theme from *Chariots of Fire*
Trois Gymnopedies (First Movement)
Theme from *The Cosmos* (Heaven and Hell) Vangelis
Theme from *The Deer Hunter* (Cavatina)

Choral

Handel's Messiah no. 147 Jesu, Joy of Man's Desiring
sung by the choir of St John's College, Cambridge
When rising from the bed of death Words: Joseph
Addison, Music: Thomas Tallis Sung by the choir of
Salisbury Cathedral
O Thou Who Camest From Above Words: Charles Wesley
Music: Samuel Wesley Sung by the Choir of Salisbury
Cathedral
My God I Love The St Francis Xavier Sung by choir of
Salisbury Cathedral

Vivaldi: Gloria in D major: *Gloria in excelsis*
Et in terra pax
Domine deus

Hymns sung by the choir of Exeter Cathedral:

Thine be the glory
King of glory, king of peace
Thee, Lord before the close of day